The Coming
Swarm

ADDITIONAL PRAISE FOR
THE COMING SWARM

The Coming Swarm

Swarm

DDoS Actions, Hacktivism, and Civil Disobedience on the Internet

MOLLY SAUTER

Bloomsbury Academic
An imprint of Bloomsbury Publishing Inc

B L O O M S B U R Y
NEW YORK · LONDON · NEW DELHI · SYDNEY

Bloomsbury Academic

An imprint of Bloomsbury Publishing Inc

1385 Broadway	50 Bedford Square
New York	London
NY 10018	WC1B 3DP
USA	UK

www.bloomsbury.com

Bloomsbury is a registered trade mark of Bloomsbury Publishing Plc

First published 2014

Library of Congress Cataloging-in-Publication Data
Sauter, Molly.
The coming swarm: DDoS actions, hacktivism, and civil disobedience
on the Internet/by Molly Sauter.
pages cm
Includes bibliographical references and index.
ISBN 978-1-62356-822-1 (hardback) – ISBN 978-1-62356-456-8 (paperback)
1. Internet–Political aspects. 2. Denial of service attacks–Political aspects.
3. Hacktivism. 4. Civil disobedience. 5. Cyberspace–Political aspects. I. Title.
HM851.S2375 2014
302.23'1–dc23
2014018645

ISBN: HB: 978-1-6235-6822-1
     PB: 978-1-6235-6456-8
     ePDF: 978-1-6289-2153-3
     ePub: 978-1-6289-2152-6

Typeset by Deanta Global Publishing Services, Chennai, India
Printed and bound in the United States of America

To my parents, Beth and Eric, for believing
studying the internet is a real thing.

CONTENTS

ACKNOWLEDGMENTS

The seed for this book was planted 4 years ago, when I was a research assistant at the Berkman Center for Internet and Society. Since then, I've been the lucky recipient of support and guidance from amazing communities without whom this book would not have existed. I could never properly thank or acknowledge everyone who helped me on the journey, but this section is an attempt to do just that. Any omissions are inadvertent, and any mistakes or errors within the text of this book are mine alone.

When Operation Payback went down in December of 2010, I was working as Jonathan Zittrain's research assistant at the Berkman Center. I will always be grateful to Jonathan for bringing me to Cambridge, and for the faith and support he has given me over the past 4 years. I hope I have lived up to it.

The Berkman Center is one of the most wonderful intellectual communities I have ever been a part of. I've been an intern, a research assistant, a Fellow, and a research affiliate here, and I am deeply honored and grateful to be able to consider the Berkman Center an intellectual home. In particular, the Berkman Fellows Hacker Culture Reading Group gave me a chance to inflict my background reading on my friends, and so I'd like to thank Kendra Albert, Ryan Budish, Jonathon Penney, Andy Sellars, Diana Kimball, and Kit Walsh for joining me in talking through so many of the issues that became central to this book without their even knowing.

This book was born from my time and work at the Comparative Media Studies Program at MIT. James Paradis, Sasha Costanza-Chock, and William Urrichio provided advice, support, and feedback throughout my time at CMS, helping to shape this and other projects. The 2013 cohort was nearly laughably codependent, but there's no one else I would rather have made that strange slog with. I am especially grateful for the long conversations and coworking sessions with Amar Boghani, Katie Edgerton, Chris Peterson, and Ayse Gursoy. Jess Tatlock and Shannon Larkin made sure that none of the graduate students in CMS starved or missed important deadlines, for which we are eternally grateful.

The Center for Civic Media became my second intellectual base in Cambridge. My cohortmates, in particular, J. Nathan Matias and Charlie De Tar, were brilliant brainstorming partners and late-night coworkers. They have consistently humbled me with their knowledge and generosity. Lorrie Lejune kept the ship of Civic sailing, provided warm blankets for naps, and a rocking chair for Life Talks. Civic provided the intellectual space for this project to develop. Ethan, Lorrie, Nathan, Charlie, Erhardt Graeff, Matt Stempeck, and Kate Darling made that space feel like a home.

I have been extraordinarily lucky to know Ethan Zuckerman, my advisor and the head of the Center for Civic Media at the MIT Media Lab. Without Ethan's intellectual generosity, guidance, faith, wisdom, and pep talks, this project would have turned out to be very different. I am grateful to know Ethan, and am proud to call him my friend. Thanks for believing there was a there here.

Some sections of this book were previously published in essay form. Zeynep Tufekci edited the essay that ultimately became Chapter 6, and her guidance was invaluable as I navigated the peer review process for the first time. Josh Glenn published my original short essay on the Guy Fawkes mask on HiLoBrow. Both Zeynep and Josh's insights ultimately helped to shape the final form of this book.

In the summer of 2012, I was fortunate enough to intern with the Electronic Frontier Foundation (EFF), where I had the chance to research sentencing practices related to Computer Fraud and Abuse Act (CFAA) violations. I'd like to thank Hanni Fakhoury, Rainey Reitman, and everyone else at the EFF for giving me that opportunity.

Since moving to Montreal to pursue my doctorate, I have been deeply grateful for the support and guidance of my advisor, Gabriella Coleman, as well as that of Darin Barney and Carrie Rentschler, and the rest of the faculty in Communication Studies at McGill University. Their perspectives have allowed this manuscript to grow beyond the scope possible at MIT.

Parts of this book were presented in draft form at PCA/ACA in Boston, HOPE Number Nine in New York, 29c3 in Hamburg, at the Berkman Center, at the Yale ISP Project, and at the Inamori Center at Case Western University. The attendees at these talks had sharp and observant questions and comments, all of which strengthened this manuscript.

Deb Chachra, Andrew Sempere, Nancy Baym, Anindita Sempere, Sarah Jeong, John Le Boeuf-Little, Rey Junco, Anna Feigenbaum, Quinn Norton, Anna Hoffman, Sean Bonner, Tanya Lokot, danah boyd, and others provided advice and insight in 140 character chunks, over e-mail, and sometimes even in person. I'm grateful to my internet community, who are supportive, funny, engaging, and always ready to provide emergency pictures of cute cats.

This book has benefited from many beta readers who generously gave their time to read and comment on the manuscript in its various forms. Kate Crawford, Josh Glenn, Jonathan Zittrain, Sasha Costanza-Chock, Biella Coleman, Astra Taylor, Willow Brugh, Jonathon Penney, Tim Maly, Jeremy Bendik-Keymer, Flourish Klink, Chia Evers, Douglas Rushkoff, Christina Xu, Leslie Kauffman, Alix Lambert, Kenneth Martin, Jason Grote, Warren Ellis, Douglas Wolk, Jordan Ellenberg, and Laurie Penny made up my Volunteer Beta Reader Army, and their comments, support, and kind readerly presence were invaluable. Thanks for encouraging me to take the rings off and fight through the thorns to the rose that was in there somewhere.

I'd also like to acknowledge the helpful comments of the anonymous peer reviewers who reviewed this book at its proposal and draft stages. Their comments and suggestions helped enormously.

Matthew Kopel, my editor at Bloomsbury, has been incredibly supportive over the past year as I transformed this body of work into a book. I'm grateful to him for his advice, guidance, and patience, and for our meetings that always seemed to involve Szechuan food.

This project, and indeed my academic career thus far, would have been impossible without the support of my family. My parents, Beth Olanoff and Eric Sauter, and my brother, Aaron Sauter, have stood behind me through my various wanderings in and out of academia, as I moved deeper into subjects that I suspect didn't always make the most sense. My parents have always trusted my brother and me to figure out our own paths, and I'm grateful for that trust.

Finally, I'd like to thank the activists and hackers who are engaged every day in the activism that this book examines. Thank you for sharing your experiences with me, correcting my misperceptions, and listening to my thoughts and theories.

FOREWORD BY ETHAN ZUCKERMAN

A university is a fine place to pick a fight.

Don't be fooled by the quiet of stately buildings, the whispering trees. Beneath the buzz of classrooms, the rustle of pages, the hum of the hallways, listen and you'll hear the underlying music of the university: the sound of argument. If the goal of academic life is knowledge, argument is the best documented path to that goal.

(And if the goal is something other than knowledge—perhaps status, security, or employment in perpetuity—these are fine topics for sparking arguments as well.)

A week into her career at MIT—3 months into mine—Molly Sauter came into my office and picked a fight. Specifically, she picked a fight with me on an issue I thought I knew inside and out: the ethical standing of a form of online protest, the denial of service attack.

I had recently finished an extended report on distributed denial of service attacks (DDoS), where multiple computers flood an internet server with traffic in order to silence it, and I felt pretty confident about my position that DDoS was A Bad Thing. My research demonstrated that these attacks, once mounted by online extortionists as a form of digital protection racket, were increasingly being mounted by governments as a way of silencing critics. They were an especially insidious form of government censorship, particularly offensive in that they were difficult to attribute to any agency and easy to deny, allowing governments to silence speech while avoiding accusations of censorship.

DDoS attacks also violate one of the best-known maxims of freedom of speech. As Justice Louis Brandeis wrote in his concurrence on Whitney v California (1927):

> To courageous, self-reliant men, with confidence in the power of free and fearless reasoning applied through the processes of popular government, no danger flowing from speech can be deemed clear and present unless the incidence of the evil apprehended is so imminent that it may befall before there is opportunity for full discussion. If there be time to expose through discussion the falsehood and fallacies, to avert the evil by the processes of education, the remedy to be applied is more speech, not enforced silence.

Or, as it's more pithily remembered, "The remedy for bad speech is more speech." The enforced silence of the DDoS attack doesn't permit us to uncover falsehoods and fallacies, which should make us suspicious that these are techniques favored by those afraid of defending their ideas in an open argument.

Over the 2 years Molly and I have worked together, she has persuaded me to consider online protest, and denial of service in particular, in a different light. While Molly acknowledges the many ways in which denial of service attacks are "impure dissent," less ethically neat in practice than they are often presented in analogies, they are, according to her, a response to a key shortcoming of the contemporary internet, the absence of public space.

Yochai Benkler and others hope that the internet will emerge as a digital public sphere, inviting arguments that are more diverse, multifaceted, and participatory than the two-sided, partisan conversations so common in the broadcast age. But the danger of the digital public sphere is not exclusion but invisibility. As Herbert Simon observed, a surplus of information leads to a surfeit of attention; in a digital public sphere, anyone can speak, but not everyone can be heard.

The most pressing threat to online speech may be the one Jerome Barron warned of in 1967. Without a right to be heard—which Barron characterizes, consistent with the media of the time, as a right of access to the press—First Amendment protections of the right to free speech may be ineffective. Protecting a right to protest where protesters are guaranteed not to be heard (now common in the Orwellian "free speech zones" erected at American political conventions) does little to enable the public political debate necessary for an open society.

In physical space, activists demand an audience by occupying public, or quasi-public space. The Civil Rights Movement boycotted buses and occupied lunch counters to demand equality of access to these places. One of Molly's key contributions in this book is the exploration of the idea that there is no public space on our contemporary internet, only complex, nested chains of private spaces. We might protest corporate malfeasance in the physical world by demonstrating on the public sidewalk outside the respective corporation's headquarters. But there are no sidewalks in online spaces, and the online alternative of creating a protest website that no one will see is an insufficient remedy. Problematic as it is, occupying a corporation's website is a way to ensure that dissent finds a relevant audience.

Ultimately, Molly's argument isn't about the technicalities of online protest technologies, though this book is an excellent introduction to that complex and fascinating space. The reason her book is critical reading even for those whose main focus is not the internet is that the questions she tackles are core to understanding the future of argument and debate. While the dangers of polarization to political discourse in America are starting to become apparent, the deeper worry is that we are moving toward a surfeit of spaces where people can express their opinions and the near absence of spaces where we are forced to encounter voices we do not choose to hear. Molly's book is less a defense of those who silence online speech than it is a plea to consider the consequences of engineering a space where protest is near invisible and impactful dissent near impossible.

We value civic arguments, whether they unfold in the halls of government, a protest encampment, or the comments thread of an internet post, because we believe in the power of deliberation. We elect representatives rather than vote directly on legislation because we hope, perhaps in vain, that the debates our legislators engage in will help us craft solutions more nuanced and balanced than they might propose in isolation. And if these arguments don't lead to finding common ground with our rivals, at least they can sharpen our positions, revealing what's weak about our own stances and positions.

The best arguments aren't the ones that lead to a compromise or resolution. They are the ones that transform those involved. I am a better scholar and a better person after 2 years of sparring intellectually with Molly, less certain that my positions are the right ones, but more sure of which priorities and beliefs are core. Molly Sauter wants to pick a fight with you, and you should be grateful for the opportunity.

Introduction: Searching for the digital street

On November 28, 2010, Wikileaks, along with the *New York Times*, *Der Spiegel*, *El Pais*, *Le Monde*, and *The Guardian* began releasing documents from a leaked cache of 251,287 unclassified and classified US diplomatic cables, copied from the closed Department of Defense network SIPRnet.[1] The US government was furious. In the days that followed, different organizations and corporations began distancing themselves from Wikileaks. Amazon WebServices declined to continue hosting Wikileaks' website, and on December 1, removed its content from its servers.[2] The next day, the public could no longer reach the Wikileaks website at wikileaks.org; Wikileaks' Domain Name System (DNS) provider,[i] EveryDNS, had dropped the site from its entries on December 2, temporarily making the site inaccessible through its URL (Associated Press, 2010). Shortly thereafter, what would be known as the "Banking Blockade" began, with PayPal, PostFinance, MasterCard, Visa, and Bank of America refusing to process online donations to Wikileaks, essentially halting the flow of monetary donations to the organization.[3]

---

[i]DNS is a hierarchical distributed naming system used to identify and locate computers connected to the internet or any networked system. One of its primary functions is to translate human-friendly URLs (such as www. wikileaks.org) into numerical IP addresses (such as 108.162.233.13). Without a DNS provider, such translations would not occur, and a website would only be accessible via the numerical IP address.

Wikileaks' troubles attracted the attention of Anonymous, a loose group of internet denizens, and in particular, a small subgroup known as AnonOps, who had been engaged in a retaliatory distributed denial of service (DDoS) campaign called Operation Payback, targeting the Motion Picture Association of America and other pro-copyright, antipiracy groups since September 2010.[4] A DDoS action is, simply, when a large number of computers attempt to access one website over and over again in a short amount of time, in the hopes of overwhelming the server, rendering it incapable of responding to legitimate requests. Anons, as members of the Anonymous subculture are known, were happy to extend Operation Payback's range of targets to include the forces arrayed against Wikileaks and its public face, Julian Assange. On December 6, they launched their first DDoS action against the website of the Swiss banking service, PostFinance. Over the course of the next 4 days, Anonymous and AnonOps would launch DDoS actions against the websites of the Swedish Prosecution Authority, EveryDNS, Senator Joseph Lieberman, MasterCard, two Swedish politicians, Visa, PayPal, and Amazon.com, and others, forcing many of the sites to experience at least some amount of downtime.[5]

For many in the media and public at large, Anonymous' December 2010 DDoS campaign was their first exposure to the use of this tactic by activists, and the exact nature of the action was unclear. Was it an activist action, a legitimate act of protest, an act of terrorism, or a criminal act? These DDoS actions—concerted efforts by many individuals to bring down websites by making repeated requests of the websites' servers in a short amount of time—were covered extensively by the media. As will be discussed in Chapter 3, this coverage was inconsistent in its characterization but was open to the idea that these actions could be legitimately political in nature. In the eyes of the media and public, Operation Payback opened the door to the potential for civil disobedience and disruptive activism on the internet. But Operation Payback was far from the first use of DDoS as a tool of activism. Rather, DDoS actions have been in use for over two decades, in support of activist campaigns ranging from pro-Zapatistas actions to protests against German immigration policy and trademark enforcement disputes.

The aim of this work is to place DDoS actions, including Operation Payback, in a historical and theoretical context, covering the use of the tactic, its development over time, and its potential for ethical political practice. Guiding this work is the overarching question of how civil disobedience and disruptive activism can be practiced in the current online space. The internet acts as a vital arena of communication, self-expression, and interpersonal organizing. When there is a message to convey, words to get out, people to organize, many will turn to the internet as the zone of that activity. Online, people sign petitions, investigate stories and rumors, amplify links and videos, donate money, and show their support for causes in a variety of ways. But as familiar and widely accepted activist tools—petitions, fundraisers, mass letter writing, call-in campaigns and others—find equivalent practices in the online space, is there also room for the tactics of disruption and civil disobedience that are equally familiar from the realm of street marches, occupations, and sit-ins?

The overwhelmingly privatized nature of the internet is a challenge to the practice of activism online, on the levels of large-scale peaceable assembly, freedom of expression, and civil disobedience. Early practitioners of DDoS actions recognized this, and staged their actions, in part, with the goal of legitimating, through practice, civil disobedience online. However, their actions did not stop continued, successful efforts by corporate, state, and regulatory powers to render the internet a privately controlled space, similar to the "privately-controlled public spaces" that pepper our physical cities today, such as Zucotti Park, the home of the original Occupy Wall Street encampment.[6] In this frame of privatization, disruptive activism is forced into conflict with the rights of private property holders, the rights and philosophies of free speech fighting with deeply engrained property rights of individuals and companies. In the physical world, activists can take their actions to the street, a culturally respected and legally protected avenue for the outpouring of civic sentiment of all kinds, be it the 1963 March on Washington or the Nationalist Socialist Party of America on the streets of Skokie. There is no "street" on the internet.

Because of this all-encompassing privatization and other reasons to be explored in this work, the theoretical and practical challenges faced by those seeking to engage in collective action, civil disobedience or disruptive activism online are different from those faced by activists organizing similarly motivated actions in the physical world. However, the two domains are often treated as though they were the same. Infringement on the property rights of private actors is often brought up as a criticism of DDoS actions, as if there was a space online that wasn't controlled by one private entity or another. Charges of censorship are usually thrown into the mix as well, because (ironically) of the internet's overwhelming use as an outlet for speech, by individuals, corporations, states, and everyone else. "Why," the critique goes, "can't you come up with a way to protest that doesn't step on somebody else's toes?" But the internet, as it were, is all somebody else's toes.

Collectively, we have allowed the construction of an entire public sphere, the internet, which by accidents of evolution and design, has none of the inherent free speech guarantees we have come to expect. Dissenting voices are pushed out of the paths of potential audiences, effectively removing them from the public discourse. There is nowhere online for an activist to stand with her friends and her sign. She might set up a dedicated blog—which may or may not ever be read—but it is much harder for her to stand collectively with others against a corporate giant in the online space. Because of the densely intertwined nature of property and speech in the online space, unwelcome acts of collective protest become also acts of trespass.

While disruptive activist actions such as DDoS actions are condemned for being an unreasonable violation of others' rights, they are also derided as being too easy. This "slacktivist" critique posits that most tools of digital activism, from disruptive tactics such as DDoS actions to changing your Facebook profile picture to proclaim your support of a cause, are lazy, simplistic modes of engagement that have little real effect on activist causes, and as such have no value. As Malcolm Gladwell articulates it in his critique of "slacktivism," which he refers to as internet-based, "weak-ties" activism,

> In other words, Facebook activism succeeds not by motivating people to make a real sacrifice but by motivating them to do the things that people do when they are not motivated enough to make a real sacrifice. We are a long way from the lunch counters of Greensboro. [North Carolina, 1960][7]

Oxblood Ruffin, one of the founding members of the influential hacktivist organization Cult of the Dead Cow, made a similar critique of Anonymous' use of DDoS:

> I've heard DDoSing referred to as the digital equivalent of a lunch counter sit-in, and quite frankly I find that offensive. It's like a cat burglar comparing himself to Rosa Parks. Implicit in the notion of civil disobedience is a willful violation of the law; deliberate arrest; and having one's day in court. There is none of that in DDoSing. By comparison to the heroes of the Civil Rights Movement DDoSing tactics are craven.[8]

Evegeny Morozov has similarly called internet-based activism "the ideal type of activism for a lazy generation," explicitly contrasting these actions to sit-ins and other iconic protest actions in past that involved "the risk of arrest, police brutality, or torture."[9]

These critiques make a series of assumptions about the purpose and practice of activism and often ground themselves historically in the Civil Rights Movement and anti-Vietnam War protests.[ii] In this model, worthwhile activism is performed on the streets, where the activist puts himself in physical and legal peril to support his ideals. Activism is "hard," not just *anyone* can do it. Activism has a strong, discernible effect on its target. If the activist is not placing herself in physical danger to express her views, then it is not valid activism.

The "slacktivist" critique achieves its rhetorical purpose by holding a developing, theoretically juvenile body of activist practices in comparison with the exceptional activist movements of the past. But it fails to consider that activism can have many divergent goals beyond direct influence on power structures. It explicitly denies that impact on individuals and personal performative identification with communities of interest can be valid activist outcomes. It demands a theoretical and practical maturity from a sphere of activism (i.e., online activism) that has not been around long enough to either adapt the existing body of theory and practice to the online environment or generate its own. It casts as a failure the fact that the simpler modes of digitally based activism allow more people to engage. As the cost of entry-level engagement goes down, more people will engage. Some of those people will continue to stay involved with activist causes and scale the ladder of engagement to more advanced and involved forms of activism. Others won't. But there must be a bottom rung to step on, and so-called slacktivism can serve as that in the online activist space.

Activist DDoS actions are easy to criminalize in the eye of the public. In fact, the majority of DDoS actions reported in the news media *are* criminal actions. DDoS is a popular tactic of extortion, harassment, and silencing. Here is another challenge faced by practitioners of activist DDoS actions not

---

[ii]This mode of critique will be addressed more specifically in Chapter 1.

faced by individuals participating in other types of disruptive actions: a sit-in is perceived as activist in nature, a DDoS action is perceived as criminal. Sit-ins are overwhelmingly used in activist situations. DDoS is deployed as a tactic of criminality much more than it is as a tactic of activism. This means that each use of DDoS as an activist tactic must first prove that it is not criminal before it can be accepted as activism. This raises vexing questions about the use of multipurpose tactics in activism when they are also effective criminal tactics. Is it possible for DDoS to be taken seriously as a tool of activism when it must first overcome such a strong association with criminality?

These negative associations and assumptions are further entrenched by the terminology commonly used to refer to DDoS actions of all stripes: DDoS *attacks*. By referring to all DDoS actions, regardless of motivation as "attacks," the public, law enforcement, and even practitioners are primed to think of DDoS actions in terms of violence, malice, and damage. In order to conduct and present this analysis without this bias toward an interpretation of violence and harm, I do not use the term "DDoS attacks" throughout this book, but rather refer to all uses of DDoS as "DDoS actions."

Today's DDoS actions are part of a history of denial of service (DoS) actions. Actions such as strikes, work slowdowns, blockades, occupations, and sit-ins all serve as ideological and theoretical antecedents to the digitally based DDoS action. Activist DDoS actions have undergone basic shifts in practice, purpose, and philosophy over the last two decades. Beginning as an exercise by experienced activists looking to stake out the internet as a new zone of action, it is now mainly practiced by transgressive, technologically mediated subcultures, often focused on internet-centered issues, who consider the online space to be a primary zone of socialization, communication, and activism. This has had implications for the basic sets of motives behind actions, the technological affordances present in the tools used, and the specific contexts of the tactics' deployment.

The structure of this work

This book will situate DDoS actions within the spheres of both online and off-line activism, addressing its development over the last two decades, and the particular aspects and challenges that separate it from similar types of disruptive activism in the physical world. Through this analysis, I address the broader issue of civil disobedience and the practice of disruptive activism in the online space. The internet is a vibrant outlet for innovative political speech, and civil disobedience is a valuable and well-respected tool of activism. This work attempts to put forward an analysis that will aid in the practice of civil disobedience on the internet, its perception as a valid form of contemporary political activism, and of the online space as an appropriate zone for disruptive political speech and action.

I begin with two brief notes, which will explain some of the technical and legal aspects of DDoS actions.

Chapter 1 positions DDoS actions within the theory and history of civil disobedience particularly as it is practiced in Western democracies. Here I argue that DDoS actions fits within the legal and theoretical framework that supports the "moral rights" understanding of modern civil disobedience and disruptive activism, and that critiques of disruptive activist practice, which base themselves in historical comparisons to the Civil Rights Movement and other iconic moments in activist history, are inappropriate and ultimately discourage innovation in political activism.

Chapter 2 examines several activist DDoS actions that fit into the category of *direct action*. These are those actions that seek to disrupt a specific process or event first and secondarily to trigger a cascade of responses on technological, political, media, and social levels. Direct action DDoSes give us an opportunity to examine issues of place in digital activism, and to address criticisms that compare DDoS actions to censorship.

Chapter 3 looks at how activist DDoS actions are covered by the media and how some groups have used these actions to explicitly funnel media attention to a particular cause. The chapter discusses different strategies groups have used to deal with the media and how successful these have been. This chapter also addresses some criticisms specifically directed at media-oriented DDoS actions, including the Critical Art Ensemble's (CAE) principal critique that such acts of "symbolic protest" were, in the online space, fundamentally ineffectual.

Chapter 4 looks closely at how activist DDoS actions contribute to the identity construction of individual activists within the collective action and the surrounding culture. Here I use Doug McAdam's concept of *biographical impact* to analyze how participating in an internet-based collective action like a DDoS could foster the development of a political activist identity.

Chapter 5 follows the previous chapter to discuss issues of identity, anonymity, and responsibility within a DDoS action. This is an attempt to bring to the fore the tensions of identity, responsibility, performance, and exclusion that sit at the core of the political use of DDoS actions. The anonymity that can be part of a DDoS action has become a particularly contentious issue among critics of DDoS actions. The construction of collective, performative identities within activist groups, especially with Anonymous, is also examined, along with issues of gender, race, and class as played out in a technologically defined activist space. Finally, this chapter explores how the concept of unsympathetic actors and "impure dissent," as defined by Tommie Shelby, applies to modern DDoS actions. These tensions exist within the use of the tactic itself and in the tactic's interplay with the political processes of a discursive democracy in general.

Chapter 6 examines the role of tool design and development in activist DDoS actions. For DDoS actions, the tool used is often serves a central, unifying function. It represents a shared jumping-off point for the action. The design and affordances of these tools can define a variety of aspects of the actions, including the level of engagement expected from participants, as well as indicating, after the fact, the types of individuals who were recruited and active, and the political "seriousness" of the action. This chapter looks at the design and development of the Electronic Disturbance Theater's (EDT) FloodNet tool, and two versions of Anonymous' Low Orbit Ion Cannon (LOIC) tool, paying particular attention to the changing functionality and interfaces of the tools.

Chapter 7 is an attempt to place the responses of corporate and state entities to activist DDoS actions in context within several trends in the regulation and governance of the online space. Here I examine how states and corporations, which are usually the targets of these activist actions, respond to DDoS actions, and the implications those responses have for free speech and emergent cyberwar policy. The result is a legal, cultural, and technical environment that chills the development of innovative technological outlets for political action and speech.

Technical note

At its most basic level, a denial-of-service action seeks to render a server unusable to anyone looking to communicate with it for legitimate purposes. When this action comes from one source, it is called a DoS, action. When it comes from multiple sources, it is called a DDoS action. Complex or sophisticated tools are not necessary to launch a DDoS action. A group of people reloading the same website again and again at the same time could constitute a manual DDoS action, if they intend to bring that site down. However, automated tools and methods are much more effective against websites that rely on today's web infrastructure.

One such automated method is to flood the target machine with "pings" from active machines. A ping is a request for availability, one computer asking another, "Are you there?"

However, when employed as part of a DDoS action, the humble ping is transformed into a "ping flood," wherein thousands of ping requests a second can be transmitted to the target server. These requests quickly overwhelm the server's limited resources, and the server is unable to effectively respond to legitimate traffic requests. This is one of the goals of the action: "downtime" on the targeted server.

A DDoS action can exploit different processes to achieve its goal, monopolizing the lines that connect the server to the outside world or taxing the target's processing and memory resources.[10] An e-mail bomb drops an enormous amount of e-mail messages onto a server, crashing it under the load. Making repeated process intensive requests, such as searches, can also cripple a website.[11]

As mentioned earlier, a few dozen people clicking "Refresh" at the same site at the same time could constitute a DDoS action. Other, far less labor-intensive ways of waging such an action exist. One method is to employ a "botnet," a collection of computers acting under the control of a central machine. Often these machines are innocents, having been illicitly infected with a program that renders them susceptible to the commands of the central machine.[12] Sometimes these are voluntary botnets, where users have volunteered their computing power by downloading and running a program. It is important to distinguish between actions carried out with botnets comprised of compromised machines, voluntary botnets, and individuals operating autonomous machines. The use of nonvolunteer botnets has a significant effect on the ethical and political validity of an activist DDoS action. This will be examined in detail in a later section.

To defend against a DDoS action is difficult and expensive. One can attempt to block the individual IP addresses the noxious traffic appears to hail from, but it is possible for a participant to spoof IP addresses, turning simple blocking into an endless game of Whac-A-Mole. If the action is distributed across a sufficiently large number of machines, the number of packets sent by each machine need not be particularly large, making it difficult to tell legitimate traffic from illegitimate. One could acquire the servers and processing power necessary to absorb the additional traffic until it abates. This avenue is generally available only to large corporations able to handle its high costs. As a result, smaller sites can sometimes be driven offline completely by a DDoS action of relatively short duration, not through the direct process of the DDoS itself but through the reactions of support services, such as internet service providers (ISPs).

Legal note

DDoS actions are considered illegal in most jurisdictions. In the United States of America, DDoS actions are prosecuted under Title 18, Section 1030 (a)(5) of the US Code.[iii] The crime described by the statute is the "intentional . . . damage" of "protected computers," which are broadly defined as

---

[iii]This section, known colloquially as the CFAA (1984), forbids any action that

> "(A) knowingly causes the transmission of a program, information, code, or command, and as a result of such conduct, intentionally causes damage without authorization, to a protected computer;
> (B) intentionally accesses a protected computer without authorization, and as a result of such conduct, recklessly causes damage; or
> (C) intentionally accesses a protected computer without authorization, and as a result of such conduct, causes damage and loss.

A "protected computer" is defined in Title 18, Section 1030 (e)(2) as

> a computer—(A) exclusively for the use of a financial institution or the United States Government, or, in the case of a computer not exclusively for such use, used by or for a financial institution or the United States Government and the conduct constituting the offense affects that use by or for the financial institution or the Government; or (B) which is used in interstate or foreign commerce or communication, including a computer located outside the United States that is used in a manner that affects interstate or foreign commerce or communication of the United States."

computers used, in whole or in part, by financial institutions or the US government. However, as will be discussed later, confusion persists about the legal status of activist DDoS actions, something that presents serious challenges to the organizers of these actions.

There are many confluences of computational circumstances that appear identical in form to a DoS or DDoS action but that are not DDoS actions. For example, a website operator may use an automated "stress-testing" tool to generate an exceptional amount of traffic directed at a particular server to test how the machine reacts, essentially launching a DoS action against his or her own machine for research purposes. There is no difference between the basic functionality of a stress-testing tool and an automated DDoS tool, and most automated DDoS tools are usually distributed as stress-testing tools.[iv]

Another example of a "DDoS that is not a DDoS" would be the crash that sometimes occurs when a popular blog links to a site whose server buckles under the unexpected crush of attention. The linker did not direct his or her followers to click the link with the intention of crashing the site, as with a manual DDoS, but the effect is the same. This makes the stipulations that crimes under the CFAA be "intentional" an important one.

Similarly, identical actions that intend to knock a site off-line could be undertaken for significantly different motivations. A DDoS action may be launched against a site in an attempt to force it to remove a specific piece of content or in an effort to

---

[iv]As noted by havonsmacker (2010) at the "loiq" DDoS tool download page:

> LOIQ stands for LOIC in Qt4. It is an attempt to re-create the LOIC server stress-test tool using Qt4/C++ instead of original C#/.Net to make it available under *NIX OSes (primarily under Linux). It is released under the terms of GNU GPL 3 or later.

It is worth noting that this "a-wink-and-a-nod" method of distribution has a physical-world analogy in the sale of glass pipes in head shops "for use with tobacco only." This is seldom their ultimate use case. (Thanks to Ethan Zuckerman for pointing out this parallel.)

drive a vulnerable site offline entirely by making it impossible for an ISP to host the content. Online publications and small ISPs are particularly vulnerable to this type of action. An example of this occurred in 1997, when a large, popularly supported DDoS campaign was launched against the ISP Institute for Global Communications (IGC)[13] in an effort to force it to stop hosting a Basque web publication, *Euskal Herria Journal*.[14] IGC's servers were knocked off-line, rendering inaccessible the websites and e-mail of more than 13,000 subscribers. Although IGC did eventually remove the *Euskal Herria Journal*'s content from its servers, it replaced it with a statement decrying what it saw as vigilante censorship on the internet and was supported in its arguments by groups such as NetAction, Computer Professionals for Social Responsibility, and the Association for Progressive Communications.[15] When classifying these types of actions, it is useful to consider the centrality of an online presence to the target's mission. To take an ISP or a small blog off-line can effectively destroy that organization or individual's ability to fulfill its professional purpose and communicate with the public. These cases might be viewed as instances of cybercrime, cyberterrorism, or censorship, and will be discussed in detail later.

Alternatively, a DDoS may be launched against a large, well-defended corporate or government site, one unlikely to fall under the pressures of a DDoS action, for the purpose of drawing attention to an issue. Such corporate or governmental homepages rarely serve a vital role in the operations of those organizations. One does not go to www.starbucks.com to get one's morning latte. Furthermore, such organizations use established press channels to communicate with the public, not poorly trafficked homepages that more often than not serve a placeholder or trademark defense purpose. To briefly tear down the online poster of these organizations[16] may serve a symbolic purpose and be a good way to attract attention, but it often has little effect on their practical, day-to-day operations. Actions aimed against such sites can be seen as an example of "electronic civil disobedience" (ECD) or valid online protest.[17] The US statute, however, contains no provisions acknowledging that such an action could constitute political speech.

The technological simplicity behind a DDoS action has contributed to its attractiveness as an activist tactic. One does not need advanced technical skills to construct a simple automated DDoS tool and virtually no skills to participate in a manual DDoS. A DDoS action also lends itself conceptually to metaphors and comparisons to physical-world activism. Activists have often called DDoS actions "virtual sit-ins." By invoking this metaphor, they seek to take advantage of the cultural capital and symbolism of historical sit-in campaigns.[18] This comparison is imperfect yet commonly invoked. The virtual sit-in metaphor is just one of a number of models and metaphors used by the tactics proponents and critics to conceptualize DDoS within existing activist practice. The use of DDoS as a protest tactic has evolved as the political identity of the internet has grown more complex. Before the use of this tactic can be understood, the tactic's place in the overall culture of digital activism must be understood.

Notes

1   Julian Borger, and David Leigh, "Siprnet: Where America stores its secret cables. Defence department's hidden Internet is meant to be secure, but millions of officials and soldiers have access," *Guardian*, November 28, 2010. Last accessed March 3, 2014, http://www.guardian.co.uk/world/2010/nov/28/siprnet-america-stores-secret-cables.

2   Jeremy Pelofsky, "Amazon stops hosting WikiLeaks website," *Reuters*, December 2, 2010. Last accessed March 3, 2014, http://www.reuters.com/article/2010/12/02/us-wikileaks-amazon-idUS-TRE6B05EK20101202.

3   Christopher Hope, "WikiLeaks' money woes brings end to leak of secrets," *Daily Telegraph*, October 24, 2011. Last accessed March 3, 2014, http://www.telegraph.co.uk/news/worldnews/

wikileaks/8845294/WikiLeaks-money-woes-brings-end-to-leak-of-secrets.html.

4 Nate Anderson, "Operation Payback attacks to go on until we 'stop being angry,'" *Ars Technica*, September 30, 2010. Last accessed February 27, 2014, http://arstechnica.com/tech-policy/news/2010/09/operation-payback-attacks-continue-until-we-stop-being-angry.ars.

5 Sean-Paul Correll, "Tis the season of DDoS: WikiLeaks edition," *PandaLabs Blog*, December 15, 2010. Last accessed February 25, 2014, http://pandalabs.pandasecurity.com/tis-the-season-of-DDoS-wikileaks-editio/.

6 Lisa Foderaro, "Privately Owned Park, Open to the Public, May Make Its Own Rules," *New York Times*, October 13, 2011.

7 Malcolm Gladwell, "Small Change: Why the Revolution Will Not Be Tweeted," *The New Yorker*, October 4, 2010.

8 Oxblood Ruffin, "Old School Hacker Oxblood Ruffin Discusses Anonymous and the Future of Hacktavism," *Radio Free Europe/Radio Liberty*, April 26, 2013. Last accessed March 3, 2014, http://www.rferl.org/content/hacker_oxblood_ruffin_discusses_anonymous_and_the_future_of_hacktivism/24228166.html.

9 Evgeny Morozov, "Foreign Policy: Brave New World of Slacktivism," *NPR*, May 19, 2009. Last accessed March 3, 2014, http://www.npr.org/templates/story/story.php?storyId104302141.

10 W. Eddy, "RFC 4987: TCP SYN flooding attacks and common mitigations," August 2007. Last accessed March 3, 2014, https://tools.ietf.org/html/rfc4987.

11 Ethan Zuckerman, Hal Roberts, Ryan McGrady, Jillian York, and John Palfrey, *2010 Report on Distributed Denial of Service (DDoS) Attacks* (Berkman Center for Internet and Society Research Publication No. 2010–16) (Cambridge, MA: Berkman Center for Internet and Society, 2010).

12 Zuckerman, et al., *2010 Report on DDoS Attacks*.

13 Institute for Global Communications, "Statement on the suspension of the Euskal Herria Journal website." July 18, 1997. Last accessed February 25, 2014. Originally published at http://www.igc.org/ehj/. Retrieved from http://www.elmundo.es/navegante/97/julio/18/igc-ehj-en.html.

14 Chris Nicol, "Internet censorship case study: *Euskal Herria Journal*," Melville, South Africa: Association for Progressive Communications. Last accessed February 25, 2014. Retrieved from http://europe.rights.apc.org/cases/ehj.html.

15 Institute for Global Communications, "Statement on the suspension of the Euskal Herria Journal website." July 18, 1997. Last accessed February 25, 2014. Originally published at http://www.igc.org/ehj/. Retrieved from http://www.elmundo.es/navegante/97/julio/18/igc-ehj-en.html.

16 Randall Munroe, "CIA," *XKCD*, August 1, 2011. Last accessed February 25, 2014. Retrieved from http://xkcd.com/932/.

17 Caroline Auty, "Political hacktivism: Tool of the underdog or scourge of cyberspace?" *ASLIB Proceedings: New Information Perspectives*, 56 (2004): 212–21; Critical Art Ensemble, *Electronic Civil Disobedience and Other Unpopular Ideas* (Brooklyn, NY: Autonomedia, 1996), 10–11.

18 Brett Rolfe, "Building an electronic repertoire of contention," *Social Movement Studies*, 4 (2005): 65–74.

CHAPTER ONE

DDoS and Civil Disobedience in historical context

". . . in a democracy, we should all be equally uncomfortable."[1]

Henry David Thoreau indirectly coined the term "civil disobedience" in a series of essays first published in 1849. These essays originally titled "Resistance to Civil Government" were eventually retitled "On Civil Disobedience." Thoreau's description of the duty of citizens to refuse to allow their government to override their conscience, interwoven with his own personal narrative of refusing to pay taxes and subsequently spending the night in jail, is one of the most influential texts in the modern understanding of the role and practice of civil disobedience in a Western democracy. Thoreau's abolitionist-motivated tax dodge is hardly the earliest example of civil disobedience, however. Hannah Arendt, in her essay "Civil Disobedience," cites Socrates and the events described in the *Crito* as a foundational episode.[2]

In this chapter I will be contextualizing DDoS actions within the historical and theoretical context of civil disobedience as it is understood today. The role of disruption, both in DDoS actions and in historical instances of civil disobedience is of particular interest. It's important to recognize that the power of a DDoS action to be disruptive to the workings of its targets and the everyday lives of digital passersby is one aspect of DDoS actions that ties them most closely to the theory of civil disobedience. The focusing power of a public disruption is often considered central to the efficacy of these political actions, both those that take place in the street and online.

Along this vein, this chapter also takes on certain critiques of DDoS-as-civil-disobedience that seem to originate from an ahistorical view of the development and implementation of civil disobedience in the United States of America. I argue that the popular and media understandings of civil disobedience in Western democracies, particularly in the United States, stem from a narrativized view of iconic moments in political activism, such as the Civil Rights Movement, which do not take into account the realities faced by political movements as they develop or the particular challenges faced by activists attempting to operate in a novel environment such as the internet, where the norms and expectations of activist speech and practice are far from established. I further argue that criticisms rooted in narrativized, media-based understandings of activist movements ultimately chill innovation in political movements.

Disruption, particularly disruption of speech or "speechy" spaces such as the internet can be a complicated issue when it occurs within the context of discursive democracy. This chapter also considers the role that the disruption of speech and the resultant episodes of nonspeech can play in a discursive democracy. Drawing on the theories of Jodi Dean and others, I am here making the potentially counterintuitive argument that sometimes what is necessary for the continued functioning of a talk- and information-based democratic system is the interpolation of silence rather than the continued injection of more (perhaps) unheeded speech.

Silence and disruption in the time of constant comment

In his 1849 tract, Thoreau describes how his abolitionist principles and opposition to the Mexican-American War led to his refusal to pay taxes, an action which he considered to be the most direct form of resistance the government, and which led to his subsequent (very brief) imprisonment. Thoreau's original conception of civil disobedience included the imprisonment of the disobedient as central to its potential impact:

> Under a government which imprisons any unjustly, the true place for a just man is also a prison. The proper place to-day, the only place which Massachusetts has provided for her freer and less desponding spirits, is in her prisons, to be put out and locked out of the State by her own act, as they have already put themselves out by their principles.[3]

For Thoreau and many who came after him, the spectacle of public disobedience was incomplete without the punitive reaction from the state. Though Thoreau maintained his actions to be in service to his own conscience, he also understood that there was an audience for his actions. His refusal to pay tax, imprisonment, and particularly his writing about it later, were intended as performances of an active injustice, wherein both Thoreau and the forces of the state were both players. For Thoreau, his act of civil disobedience specifically involved inducing the state to participate in a public drama by which the state would be revealed as unjust and Thoreau confirmed as a just man with a just cause.

Similarly, Martin Luther King Jr advocated the acceptance of punishment as central to his position of nonviolent civil disobedience:

> One who breaks an unjust law must do so openly, lovingly, and with a willingness to accept the penalty. I submit

that an individual who breaks a law that conscience tells him is unjust, and who willingly accepts the penalty of imprisonment *in order to arouse the conscience of the community over its injustice*, is in reality expressing the highest respect for law.[4]

The Civil Rights Movement in the United States in the 1950s and 1960s is considered the modern paradigmatic example of collective civil disobedience by many. The highly mediated movement, photographed, filmed, and televised, cast the mold for the popular perception of civil disobedience. Stark images of peaceful street marchers beset by police dogs, lunch counter sit-ins, and Rosa Parks at the front of the bus are timeless illustrations of a righteous minority standing firm in the face of obvious injustice. Following Thoreau's model, civil disobedience during the Civil Rights Movement meant, for many activists, putting their bodies and identities on the line, getting arrested for their cause in full view of the state and the media.

This is a widely recognized script for the conduct of civil disobedient activism: it happens in public, it happens on the street, and activists willingly face consequences such as arrest or injury for their cause. It's a script the news media readily recognizes, and activists who adhere to it are rewarded with coverage that legitimates its political nature. When trying to understand modern instances of civil disobedience or disruptive activism, be it Occupy, the global justice movement, or internet-based actions such as DDoS, the Civil Rights Movement is often treated as a singular touchstone, used to determine the validity and political seriousness of the action in question. Over the last half century, the Civil Rights Movement in the United States has taken a venerated place in political history. Its history has been narrativized and packaged to the point where it has become virtually ahistorical, and no modern, developing movement could possibly stand up in comparison. Inevitably, such comparisons on the part of the media and the public serve to only stifle innovation within social movements and political action, while at the same time cultivating a deep and unproductive nostalgia for a kind of "ideal activism" that never existed. This view is reflected in the "slacktivist" critiques mentioned earlier, with the likes of social critics Malcolm Gladwell, Evegeny Morozov, and hacktivists Oxblood Ruffin explicitly (and negatively) comparing contemporary online activists to civil rights era activists.

One aspect of civil disobedience that this nostalgia glosses over is its potential for disruption. The marches, sit-ins, and boycotts of the civil rights era were intensely disruptive and were intended to be so. As Martin Luther King Jr wrote in his "Letter from a Birmingham Jail":

> Nonviolent direct action seeks to create such a crisis and foster such a tension that a community which has constantly refused to negotiate is forced to confront the issue. It seeks so to dramatize the issue that it can no longer be ignored. My citing the creation of tension as part of the work of the nonviolent resister may sound rather shocking. But I must confess that I am not afraid of the word "tension." I have earnestly opposed violent tension, but there is a type of constructive, nonviolent tension which is necessary for growth. Just as Socrates felt that it was necessary to create a tension in the mind so that individuals could rise from the bondage of myths and half truths to the unfettered realm of creative analysis and objective appraisal, so must we see the need for nonviolent gadflies to create the kind of tension in society that will help men rise from the dark depths of prejudice and racism to the majestic heights of understanding and brotherhood. The purpose of our direct action program is to create a situation so crisis packed that it will inevitably open the door to negotiation. I therefore concur with you in your call for negotiation. Too long has our beloved Southland been bogged down in a tragic effort to live in monologue rather than dialogue.[5]

In this passage, Dr King pushes for the creation of what he calls "tension," and what I would call "disruption,"[i] as the path to forcing a dialogue in the public sphere. Of course, it's easy to acknowledge the virtue of disruption in a bygone era for a movement that is universally acknowledged to have been necessary and moral. Often it's a trickier proposition to see the democratic utility of disrupting the status quo when it is *your* status quo being disrupted, by activists whose causes or tactics you might not fully understand or agree with. Legal theorist William Smith states, "It is common for democracies to celebrate figures from their *past* who used civil disobedience in campaigns to improve their institutions and society. It is less common for democracies to be explicit in acknowledging that civil disobedience *continues* to be a reasonable and sometimes justified form of political participation."[6] Dissent, particularly when it reflects unpopular, poorly understood, or poorly funded causes, often must engage in disruption of the everyday patterns of life to be heard. This is true in the physical world as well as in the online space. Without exploiting the capacity of disruption to direct the attention and political resources of a discursive democracy, it's likely that causes which do not align with values already present in the mainstream political discourse would not be addressed, or would not be addressed as valid political concerns.

The popular instinct to judge modern protest actions against the memory of the Civil Rights Movement disregards the ways in which the context and practice of activism has changed or ignores central realities of activist practice that have been present for some time. It also ignores realities about how political movements, including the Civil Rights Movement, develop, adapt, and change over time, in terms of their organizing, street tactics, and media practices. Many of the most iconic moments in the Civil Rights Movement were exquisitely stage-managed

---

[i]Here and elsewhere in this book, I use the word "disruption" to refer to actions and events that cause a breakage in the flow of normal events without causing physical destruction or physical damage to persons or property.

to maximize their media impact and to cast the movement in the most sympathetic light possible. Rebecca Wanzo notes in her book, *The Suffering Will Not Be Televised*,

> The story of Rosa Parks is one of the most iconographic stories of the Civil Rights Movement. As the tale is often told, Parks refused to give up her seat for a white man because she was "tired" and this lone woman "inspired the Civil Rights Movement." Of course, people had been working toward civil rights for a long time, and Parks was not the first woman in Montgomery to be arrested for refusing to give up her bus seat in 1955. Fifteen-year-old Claudette Colvin was arrested on March 2, nine months before Park's arrest in December. The civil rights leaders had deemed Colvin an inappropriate figurehead for the movement. She was known to spout profanity (and in fact had done so on the day of the arrest) and was an unwed pregnant teenager. In October, Mary Louise Smith refused to leave her seat for a white woman, but she was deemed an inappropriate candidate for mobilization as well because she was the very poor daughter of a man rumored to be an alcoholic. By contrast, Parks was a soft-spoken seamstress who was the secretary of the local NAACP chapter.[7]

In selecting Rosa Parks as the "figurehead" for the Montgomery Bus Boycott, civil rights leaders chose a woman who could be seen as strong, noble, and sympathetic by large swathes of the public. However, Wanzo further notes, ". . . the refusal to mobilize on behalf of citizens who cannot be framed as ideal is a characteristic of political activism that comes with significant costs."[8] Movements, and those within them, are expected to stand as idealized representations of political communities. Movements, activists and victims of harm who don't adhere to broadly sentimentalized narratives of political action can have their value as political actors rejected: "'Bad' victims like Claudette Colvin make for narrative messiness, and sentimental political storytelling rejects complex tales."[9] However the political value of individuals and social movements shouldn't be denigrated because of the inability of one or the other to adhere to prescribed standards of social sympathy.

The storytelling which occurs around social movements favors clear, emotionally compelling through-lines, which are often difficult, if not impossible to discern in the moment, on the street, or at the computer. The present is always messy, only the past has the opportunity to be clean(ed). Ongoing or developing activist actions simply cannot be consumed by the public in the same fashion as iconic social movements which have had half a century to establish narratives in the media and the public imagination. Criticism that compares the developing world of online-based activism, such as DDoS actions or "clicktavist" or "slacktivist" actions, to the sit-ins and boycotts of the Civil Rights Movement is essentially empty. Not only do these new movements and actions not have the same goals as the Civil Rights Movement, they are also not organized by activists with the same level of or same kind of experience, and they occupy entirely different historical moments, with respect to when they are taking place, when they are being examined, and how. So not only do these popular critiques often bear little relationship to how the Civil Rights Movement occurred on the ground, but they also fail to realize that a comparison between internet-based activism occurring at the turn of the millennium and the iconic ideal of the midcentury Civil Rights Movement often serves no other purpose than to fault the current generation of political activists for not being their grandparents.

Similarly, this ahistorical myopia that encourages the exile of tactics such as occupations, blockades, monkey wrenching, defacements, culture jamming, strikes, sabotage, and many more from the popularly recognized repertoire of civil disobedience discourages activism and dissent, as well as any meaningful analysis thereof. It should not be surprising that these disruptive, and in some cases destructive, tactics, often interpreted to fall outside the realm of "acceptable" political acts, are used primarily by groups that are historically underprivileged in the area of public politics. Students, blue-collar workers, inner-city youth, the homeless, those living below the poverty line, and other minorities are routinely pushed out of public political life because they are not engaging in what is popularly accepted as proper political conduct. These biases toward what "counts" as politically valid conduct and speech contributes to disenfranchisement and narrows the public political discourse. By ignoring the potential legitimacy of these out-of-the-mainstream disruptive tactics, critics are contributing to this systemic disenfranchisement by artificially and harmfully restricting what political speech and conduct is acceptable and, by extension, whose. A refusal to adapt to the modern, accepted repertoire of contention also implies a refusal to acknowledge basic changes in how the media and governments interact with political activists, particularly in the online space. Also dismissed are how the growing roles of corporations, multigovernmental organizations, and nongovernmental organizations have made these entities apt targets for performative, disruptive dissent. Traditional theories of civil disobedience often do not include anticorporate actions within the scope of "appropriate" uses of civil disobedience. However, as will be discussed in detail in Chapter 7, any attempt to fully grapple with online-based activism must include anticorporate actions as valid, given the strong (some would say dominate) role many corporations have in the governance of the online space, through influence on government and regulatory bodies as well as through code and contracts (like mandatory Terms of Service and binding arbitration clauses).

In terms of operational theory and impact, activist DDoS actions are not meaningfully different from other actions within the history of civil disobedience. What they are is novel, and they occur in a novel environment: the online space. This novelty, and their ability to impact the lives of nonparticipants at potentially unprecedented scale, contributes greatly to their controversial nature. However, novelty cannot properly exempt activist DDoS from being classified as a tactic of civil disobedience. Its disruptive nature cannot, on its own, render it inappropriate or criminal.

Nor does the nature of DDoS actions as "things which disrupt the meaning of others" render it in and of itself meaningless. Rather, the disruption itself is full of meaning. An activist DDoS action allows activists to step directly into the constantly shifting information stream and take a role in its temporary alterations. The act of reaching into and reshaping the flow of technological communications constitutes an act of political speech and conduct similar to what Bryan Pfaffenberger called "technological reconstitution." Technological reconstitution permits a theoretical structure by which activists can reshape the use, deployment, and manifestation of technologies "guided by a self-consciously 'revolutionary' ideology."[10] This reshaping produces technological "counterartifacts," which in turn make space for counter- and inverted-ideologies to occupy the technological space.[11]

Pfaffenberger's framework gives us the opportunity to break apart the impact of activist DDoS actions on the level of its technological politics. Here the counterartifact produced is the disruption itself. The blank browser screen, the long-delayed load time. By combining Pfaffenberger's concept of the counterartifact with Jodi Dean's theory of communicative capitalism, we can see how the imposition of silence and delay into a signal rich environment can be not only a powerful discursive contribution, but also a necessary one for the proper functioning of the public sphere.

The "counterartifact" produced here is the disruption itself. By replacing continuity with disruption, activists attempt to create a rhetorical cavity in the digitized structure of capitalism wherein activism can take place. This break in "business as usual" makes room for the counteractions of activism. It is the creation of excavated, disrupted space that is valuable in these contexts, sometimes even more valuable than a direct discursive engagement between activists and their target. The fact of the disruption is here the salient contribution, particularly when the moment of disruption is conceived of not as a space without content, but as a space without *signal*. In Dean's theory of communicative capitalism, she intentionally renders irrelevant the content of messages circulating within the networked data stream. Dean states that under communicative capitalism, which is the particular brand of interaction that dominates the networked environment within which our particular activity of interest solely occurs, "[m]essages are contributions to circulating content—not actions to elicit responses. The exchange value of messages overtakes their use value." She continues, "A contribution need not be understood; it need only be repeated, reproduced, forwarded. Circulation is the setting for the acceptance or rejection of a contribution."[12] In communicative capitalism, Dean argues, messages are reduced to their pure signal value, in particular to their reproducible signal value. In that context, the interruption of that signal becomes an equally powerful contribution. The interruption can be interpreted to be the only reasonable form of response to an "interlocutor," such as a government or corporation, that is, by its projected nature, fundamentally nonresponsive.

If we look at the moment of content-less interruption as a moment of impact to be absorbed rather than a conveyance of content to be understood, we can then look at it as a form of exchange between differently empowered groups or between different power structures. What is invited is not a confrontation with another, which in Dean's constant whirl of murmured content with no audience is not possible anyway. Under communicative capitalism, it is possible that it is the intentional creation of disruptions and silence that is the most powerful contribution.

The disruptions and silences that result provide a digestive reprieve from the self-referential swirl of content that demands constant comment but never makes room for reflection and analysis. It opens bandwidth for speech from new actors and participants in a public discourse that otherwise only ever receives signals from those (always) already broadcasting. The disruption inherent in DDoS actions is not empty of meaning. The targeted content is not supplanted by a void. Rather, it is exchanged for the fact of action. A conversation occurs, though the parties are speaking with different vocabularies.

The intentionality of these actions is important. Activist DDoS actions and other types of disruptive activism are not random acts of vandalism; they are not simply shouting someone down with nonsensical noise. The exchange of speech for action or speech for conduct (and the subsequent exchange of that conduct for more speech perhaps from an unfamiliar source) is still a type of conversation. Disruptive activism and most types of civil disobedience, in general, tend to be conduct-based rather than speech-based activism. Despite this (or perhaps because of it), the value and validity of conduct as a type of political participation is often doubted or distrusted. In her essay, "Civil Disobedience," Hannah Arendt quotes the US Supreme Court as saying, "'. . . conduct under the First Amendment does not enjoy the same latitude as speech does,' and 'conduct, as opposed to speech is [of course] endemic' to civil disobedience."[13] The common bias against the political value or relevance of "conduct-statements" as it were does not negate their capacity to convey strong political meaning or impact. It does, however, make the initial acceptance and interpretation difficult. As was discussed earlier, when political activism does not fit into the popularly accepted concept of what is "valid," disenfranchisement can follow. In Chapter 3, I will discuss in more detail the role of the media in determining what is or is not "valid." For now, though, it should be clear that while conduct-based political activism uses a different active vocabulary than speech-based activism, they remain in dialogue with each other.

As we look at the role of DDoS within online activism, the reader should bear in mind the power of disruption to draw attention to issues that no one wants to talk about, and to call different types of stakeholders to account. Though DDoS as a tactic is still relatively novel, it fits within a centuries-long tradition of breaking laws and disrupting business as usual to make a political point. These actions aren't simply disruption for disruption's sake. Rather they serve to help the activist or dissenter to direct the attention of the public through the interpolation of difference into routine. The activist's generation of popular discomfort through disruption facilitates the conversations and confrontations that make up a working democracy.

"Full and free discussion even of ideas we hate"

It has been put forward that in representative democracies, civil disobedience, like other forms of political speech, is a right. David Lefkowitz, William Smith, and others have described this right to engage in the practice of civil disobedience, and Lefkowitz further clarifies that it includes a "right to do wrong."[14] Lefkowitz characterizes civil disobedience as "an act of public communication of participation . . . [I]t must be reasonable for those who commit such acts to believe that by doing so they will be able to communicate to (some of) their political leaders and fellow citizens their beliefs regarding the moral acceptability of the state's current exercise of authority."[15] Lefkowitz claims that insomuch as modern deliberative democracies accept a moral right to political participation, that right includes a right to civil disobedience in so far as it is noncoercive (though not necessarily nondestructive or disruptive) and is intended to serve as a communicative act. The moral rights model covers indirect civil disobedience, or actions where the law being broken is not what is being objected to, as well as direct civil disobedience. I use Lefkowitz's moral right frame as a base for my concept of the role of civil disobedience in networked democratic societies: functionally and theoretically, acts of civil disobedience constitute acts of participation and communication, even in the face of their disruptive potential.

Central to this definition is the understanding of the protest action as part of the protester's right to political participation as well as contributing to the greater public political discourse as a whole. Civil disobedience, as previously discussed in this chapter, allows political minorities and others with limited access to the media and public sphere introduce issues into the public discourse that may otherwise be ignored. Lefkowitz views civil disobedience as, through its disruptive potential, reducing the barriers that stand in the way of certain population's full participation in the process of deliberative democracy. This includes the ability to introduce and argue issues in the public discourse as well as reacting to the arguments of others. He describes the moral right to political participation as

> . . . reduc[ing] as much as possible the degree to which it is a matter of luck whether one attracts majority support for one's reasonable views regarding what justice requires. . . . That is, respect for agents' moral right to political participation requires that potential barriers to their effective exercise of this right be diminished as much as possible.[16]

As civil disobedience and other forms of potentially disruptive yet communicative protest are reasonable forms of political participation, Lefkowitz includes a right to civil disobedience within his conception of a right to political participation.

Lefkowitz further argues that the moral right to civil disobedience partakes of a right to do so, even if the cause being advocated is wrong. To deny an individual a right to advocate for wrong, unjust, or, I would add, offensive causes renders meaningless any offers of political freedom at all; ". . . to allow agents to participate in political discussion making or to implement their decisions only when they make (what we believe to be) morally correct choices, would be to deny those agents autonomous lives—ones in which they exercise a significant degree of control over the shape and direction their lives take."[17] This interpretation means that the right of an activist to engage in civil disobedience or disruptive activism cannot be denied simply because the cause they advocate is morally wrong, distasteful, or offensive, or is interpreted by a given group of people to be so. While in practice this can be expected to impose costs on third parties, Lefkowitz argues that "people should have to bear the costs involved in others' exercise of their moral right to political participation. . . ."[18] Lefkowitz's framework describes the participatory value of civil disobedience, the right of citizens in a deliberative democracy to advocate for "wrong" causes, and the expectation that citizens should bear the cost of each other's exercising their rights to political participation. It underscores the understanding that the best expression of democratic practice is not necessarily manifest in intellectual stability and comfort, but rather in the widest distribution of opportunities for individual participation and necessary social change possible. Because this definition recognizes the imperfect distribution of these opportunities for engagement in actually existing democracies, it holds that the types of disruptive actions found under the umbrella of civil disobedience to be as central a right as other, more mainstream modes of political participation, like the anonymous ballot.

Accepting that civil disobedience is a right, how should the state react to those who engage in it? It's clear that states cannot simply accept the willful violations of laws, even if the violation was politically motivated. Ironically, this would often render the act of protest toothless as, as was discussed earlier in this chapter, the spectacle of the protestor engaged in a confrontation with the state is often central to the pageantry of civil disobedience. Here the difference between *penalization* and *punishment* becomes vital. Lefkowitz and William Smith articulate a difference in kind between the state penalizing civil disobedients and punishing them. Punishment, in the guise of harsh sanctions, long jail sentences, high fines, or changes in citizen status (such as becoming a convicted felon), serves to convey moral judgments on the actions taken and often tries to dissuade others from engaging in the same types of activities. Penalties, like token fines, arrests that do not result in criminal charges, or brief jail stays, on the other hand, do not convey a moral judgment and often hold little dissuading power.

Penalties can often be read as the state acknowledging the reality and seriousness of the protest at hand. As will be discussed later, penalizing actions of the state can often serve a legitimating purpose in protests, as the state uses its power judiciously to acknowledge that an oppositional political stance is being taken. Many activists rely on the reaction of the state to provide an opportunity to dramatize their commitment to a cause. Smith argues that the imposition of penalties after a disruptive protest can show that activists are still respectful of the public sphere and the bonds of "civic friendship" they share with other citizens.[19] Lefkowitz and Smith each argue that while the state has an interest in penalizing citizens engaged in acts of civil disobedience, any *punishment* of those citizens violates their right to political participation and ultimately damages the processes of democracy.[20]

To see how DDoS fits within Lefkowitz and Smith's theories, it is important to remember that, like other acts of civil disobedience and disruptive activism, activist DDoS actions are communicative in nature. Though they are indirect (i.e., they often break laws and disrupt services other than those they object to) and though their messaging often takes place through separate (yet closely tied) channels, these aspects do no disqualify activist DDoS actions from falling under the moral right frame described by Lefkowitz and Smith. Because of that, it is particularly revealing to look at the state responses to activist DDoS actions within their context as acts of civil disobedience. These will be examined in greater detail in a later chapter, though it is worth noting here that the most recent spate of activist DDoS actions, occurring from 2007 through 2012, mostly involving Anonymous, have prompted extremely aggressive reactions from the US government. Because of the US government's refusal to acknowledge these actions as civil disobedience and some particularities of US computer crime law, individuals arrested in connection with these actions have been threatened with up to 15 years in prison and $500,000 in fines and restitution payments. These threats surpass the regulatory function of *penalizing*, serving instead the "example-making" purpose of *punishment*, meant to dissuade others from taking up the same banners and tactics.

Here the US government appears to be exploiting these protest actions to convey a strong opposition to the use of this tactic, no matter its legitimacy as a form of activism. Prosecutors appear to be taking advantage of the uncertainly prompted by the novelty of the tactic and its environment to both strongly discourage its use and to chill any further innovation in the area of disruptive online activism and digital civil disobedience. The US government, which has over the past few decades demonstrated a strong willingness to engage in the surveillance and harassment of political activists, has an interest in discouraging the movement of activist activity to zones that enable anonymous actions across geopolitical borders, which would make it easier for activists to engage transnationally in political movements and causes, while at the same time potentially hampering US efforts to monitor and control such nonmainstream political activities.

It is the nature of the online environment itself that has made disruptive tactics such as activist DDoS actions increasingly necessary. However, the news media is still the arbiter of popular attention, deciding which activist causes are worth space on the front page or time on the 11 o'clock news. As mentioned earlier in this chapter, if the actions taken by activists don't "look like" activism, or the views presented are too outside the mainstream to appeal to viewers—and advertisers—it is likely that these actions will not be covered at all.[21] However it is vital to a democracy that unpopular and dissenting ideas be aired, discussed, and debated in the open. As Justice William O. Douglas wrote in his 1951 dissent to *Dennis v. United States*:

> Full and free discussion even of ideas we hate encourages the testing of our own prejudices and preconceptions. Full and free discussion keeps a society from becoming stagnant and unprepared for the stresses and strains that work to tear all civilizations apart. Full and free discussion has indeed been the first article of our faith.[22]

An unbroken broadcasting of the status quo impoverishes our democracy. In order to avoid such a situation, dissenting views must not only be *spoken* but also *heard*. Owen Fiss,[23] Jerome Barron,[24] and others have presented interpretations of the First Amendment that encompass a "right to be heard" and a "right to hear" as well as a "right to speak." Though it may be argued that the internet has substantially increased the number of soapboxes available, it has not increased the availability of the audience. Rather, as individuals become more adept at filtering their information taps, and as the infrastructure of the internet and the physical world around them makes it easier to avoid unwanted encounters with unpopular or simply different viewpoints, the ability of dissenters to truly have a voice in the national debate is being steadily diminished.[25]

For unpopular and dissenting causes to attract the attention of a news media industry that, for economic reasons, is often uninterested in covering them, disruption of some kind can be necessary. Attention is attracted via the fact of the disruption, and the dissenting view is covered. As mentioned earlier, this is often a complicated process as activists attempt to engage the attention of the mainstream through the use innovative and disruptive tactics, always running a risk that their activism will not be recognized as such or dismissed as a novelty. This will be discussed in greater detail in Chapter 3. In an information landscape where corporate, homogenized news media still dominates much of the agenda setting, resorting to extreme tactics in the hopes of being heard is often a better option for the dissenter than simply waiting to be heard by grace and chance, a situation, Lefkowitz notes, the moral rights model of political participation seeks to avoid. In this way, disruption is a necessary part of the modern political discourse. Online, that disruption may take the form of a DDoS action, while in the physical world it may take another, perhaps more familiar form. What is critical is that the status quo, the normal flow of information must be disrupted if dissenting voices are to be both voiced and heard.

Notes

1 Tressie McMillan Cottom, "Presenting Selves: Social Class, Gender and Intersectionality in Ethnography." October 6, 2013. Last accessed February 23, 2014, http://tressiemc. com/2013/10/06/presenting-selves-race-social-class-gender-and-intersectionality-in-ethnography/.

2 Hannah Arendt, *Crises of the Republic* (San Diego: Harcourt Brace, 1972), 51.

3 Henry David Thoreau, *Civil Disobedience* (1849). Last accessed February 25, 2014, http://thoreau.eserver.org/civil2. html.

4 Martin Luther King, Jr, "Letter from a Birmingham Jail" (1963). Last accessed February 25, 2014, http://www.africa.upenn.edu/Articles_Gen/Letter_Birmingham.html.

5 King, "Letter from a Birmingham Jail."

6 William Smith, *Civil Disobedience and Deliberative Democracy* (London: Routledge, 2013), 109.

7 Rebecca Wanzo, *The Suffering Will Not Be Televised* (Albany: SUNY Press, 2009), 29.

8 Wanzo, *The Suffering Will Not Be Televised*, 29.

9 Ibid., 30.

10 Bryan Pfaffenberger, "Technological Dramas," *Science, Technology, and Human Values* 17 (1992): 282.

11 Pfaffenberger, "Technological Dramas," 282.

12 Jodi Dean, "Technology: The Promises of Communicative Capitalism," in *Democracy and Other Neoliberal Fantasies: Communicative Capitalism and Leftist Politics* (Durham: Duke University Press, 2009), 26–7.

13 Arendt, *Crises of the Republic*, 85.

14 Smith, *Civil Disobedience and Deliberative Democracy*, 84–109; David Lefkowitz, "On a Moral Right to Civil Disobedience," *Ethics* 117 (2007): 202–33.

15 Lefkowitz, "On a Moral Right to Civil Disobedience," 215–16.

16 Ibid., 215.

17 Ibid., 228.

18 Ibid., 221.

19 Smith, *Civil Disobedience and Deliberative Democracy*, 22.

20 Ibid., 97; David Lefkowitz, "On a Moral Right to Civil Disobedience," *Ethics* 117 (2007): 203.

21 Jerome Barron, "Access to the Press—A New First Amendment Right," *Harvard Law Review* 1641 (1967): 1641–78.

22 William O. Douglas, *Dennis v. United States* (1951), 341 US. 494,584.

23 Owen Fiss, *The Irony of Free Speech* (Cambridge, MA: Harvard University Press, 1996).

24 Barron, "Access to the Press—A New First Amendment Right," 1641–78.

25 Timothy Zick, *Speech Out of Doors: Preserving First Amendment Liberties in Public Places* (Cambridge: Cambridge University Press, 2009).

CHAPTER TWO

Blockades and blockages: DDoS as direct action

In late November 1999, the World Trade Organization (WTO) held its Ministerial Conference in Seattle, Washington. The city streets were filled with protesters opposed to the WTO's procorporate globalization agenda. A number of different activist organizations were involved, and a variety of tactics were employed, running the gamut from peaceful permitted street marches, puppets and colorful costumes (including a plethora of activists dressed up as sea turtles) to the Black Bloc's highly confrontational campaign of corporate property destruction. Popularly known as the Battle for Seattle, the coming together of so many different activist groups coupled with the aggressive response of police and city officials helped make the 1999 WTO protests into a defining moment for the anticorporate globalization movement.

While the sea turtles were marching in the streets of Seattle, a British organization called *the electrohippies* waged a simultaneous online action against the WTO. From November 30 through December 4, *the electrohippies* organized and staged a combination DDoS/e-mail bombing campaign targeting the WTO's main conference servers, public-facing websites, as well as various individuals associated with the WTO, including PR and operations staff, and various state representatives.

The DDoS section of the action used a Javascript tool, based on an open source tool developed by the EDT in 1998. Technological limitations required that participants be connected to the internet with the tool, available at *the electrohippies* webpage, downloaded and running for the duration of their participation. Representatives of the group claimed that over the course of the action, over 450,000 people participated in the action, with the targeted sites experiencing sporadic downtime and service slowdowns. The extent to which the DDoS action affected the functioning of the WTO websites and conference network is disputed. The goal of the DDoS action, stated in the calls to action distributed on various mailing lists and on its website, was to hamper the PR efforts of the conference:

> [T]he *electrohippies* are organising a "virtual sit-in" of the WTO's special conference website. It is intended that this website will be the main conduit for accessing information about the conference, and the events taking place. By taking action against the conference server and the main WTO server, we restrict the PR staff at the WTO from spreading their global corporate agenda.[1]

After the DDoS campaign ended on December 4, *the electrohippies* began a 2-day e-mail bombing campaign. The group directed their supporters to e-mail large, uncompressed picture and document files (some suggested documents were the Kyoto Protocol on Climate Change, and several Environmental Protection Agency (EPA) and WHO reports) along with personal messages, to a list of WTO affiliated addresses. The goal was to overwhelm the internal e-mail systems of the organization and hamper internal communications.

> So far we've demonstrated that the WTO's public information system is not immune from public pressure. Now we move to their private information system—their email. What we would like people to do is email the WTO with personal

meepassages expressing your own reasons why you object to them and the Seattle conference. Of course, sending a short types [sic] message will not be that effective—so you'll also need to attach a large file to send with it.[2]

Four years before *the electrohippies action*, in 1994, CAE published an essay called, "Electronic Civil Disobedience" (ECD). The essay served as a call for activists to move the locus of their activism from the streets to the digital, online space: "The CAE has said it before, and we will say it again: as far as power is concerned, the streets are dead capital!"[3] Organizations and systems of power had moved from the physical world to take up residence in the networks of "cyberspace" (a term which dates the essay rather sharply), and if activists and agitators wanted to have any impact at all, they had no choice but to follow them there.

The CAE advocated directly importing "traditional" civil disobedience to the digital space. "Blocking information conduits is analogous to blocking physical locations: however, electronic blockage can cause financial stress that physical blockage cannot and it can be used beyond the local level. [Electronic civil disobedience] is [civil disobedience] invigorated. What CD once was, ECD is now."[4] They advocated direct engagement with institutions over individuals, encouraging activists to exploit the affordances of the network to make possible a direct confrontation between the activist-as-individual and the structural manifestations of power that were moving into the online space.

What tactics could be deployed, and how, became a point of contention within the CAE. Eventually, a small group of activists split from the larger organization to form the EDT, a group that will play a large role in our analysis. Right now, though, it is important to note that the CAE was advocating a type of digital direct action. Direct action, as an ideologically grounded set of tactics, values direct confrontation with oppressive structures of power. These could be state or corporate structures. The goal is to both disrupt the prevailing structure that is seen to be causing harm, and thus hopefully lessening its impact, and to provoke a response, usually unduly punitive or violent, which is then allowed to stand on its own as an illustration of the reality of the challenged institution,[5] similar to Thoreau's goal of performing the state's unjust nature by provoking his own arrest. Direct action as a motivating ideology assigns to individuals the power and the responsibility to confront and interrupt harmful systems and structures without requiring that those actions be sublimated through those systems and structures, which could imply tacit approval.

Direct action is often highly performative, engaging in both an illustration of alternative modes of political engagement, what has been referred to as "propaganda by deed"[6] and a deliberate provocation to the target. The spectacle of an unreasonable response can add resonance to the original issues the activists meant to highlight.

This chapter looks at several DDoS actions that can be categorized as direct action DDoSes. Like other direct action tactics, these DDoS actions seek first, to disrupt a process for the purpose of disrupting that process, and secondarily, to trigger a cascade of responses on technological, political, media, and social levels. The direct action DDoS most clearly highlights the importance of "place" and proximity within digital activism, a concept that this chapter will explore through the theory of "contested space." Like street direct action, direct action DDoS actions are vulnerable to charges of censorship or harassment or simply disrupting democratic conversation with meaningless noise. This chapter will also examine the merits of those critiques.

Functional metaphors of geography and physicality

The electrohippies were interested in creating models of online activism that were functionally and philosophically equivalent to physical practices already in existence. In this they weren't alone; the EDT had been running what they referred to as "virtual sit-ins" beginning in 1998. Both *the electrohippies* and the EDT were interested in establishing the online space as an arena of activism socially, culturally, and legally equivalent to the physical world. They made heavy use of the "virtual sit-in" metaphor and used "popular legitimacy" as a marker of success:

> The structure of client-side distributed actions developed by *the electrohippies* means that there must be widespread support across a country or continent in order to make the system work. Our method has built within it the guarantee of democratic accountability. If people don't vote with their modems (rather than voting with their feet) the action would be an abject failure.[i]

The "client-side" terminology used here differentiated *the electrohippies'* action from other types of DDoS actions that did not require the conscious, active commitment of a large number of participants to be successful. The "client-side" approach was philosophically conceived of as opposed to exploit-based and application layer "server-side" actions, which could amplify the flow of traffic from individual participants or use means which did not rely on the active presence of thousands of

---

[i] "Client-side Distributed Denial-of-Service: Valid campaign tactic or terrorist act?" is collectively credited to "DJNZ and the action tool development group of *the electrohippies collective*" This is further explained:

> "*the electrohippies collective* are a 'virtual group' in the sense that their activities are organised and carried out solely on the Internet *they do not meet*. The aim of the group is to extend the philosophy of activism and direct action into the 'virtual' world of electronic information exchange and communications. Why use the name 'electrohippies'? It's based upon a situationist paradox that seeks to promote a positive message by exploiting it's negative connotations. But it's also a nicely comical label, with plenty of stereotypical overtones that we can exploit as a means to make our point about the position of ordinary people within the global 'new world order.'"
> (DJNZ 2000)

participants to bring down a site. *The electrohippies*, and the EDT before them, purposefully hamstrung the technological tools they used in order to maintain a one-to-one participant to signal ratio.[7]

The desire to remain in functional lockstep with existing forms of on-the-street activism (the refusal to augment activist traffic, the strict reliance on popular participation for judgments of success) also provides a basis for the use of DDoS as a tool of direct action. *The electrohippies* viewed the internet as a public space whose ability to function as such was being compromised by the overwhelming presence of corporate and commercial interests. The WTO action was intended to hamper the public and private operation of the WTO, but also to be a forceful, public-facing statement in support of the right of the public to use the internet as a public, activist space.

In the United States, "public" space is not always necessarily public, and "private" space is, likewise, not always wholly private. Rather, the Supreme Court has repeatedly described a "continuum" of public fora, which has been aptly described by several scholars[ii] of free speech and public activism. The continuum roughly articulates four types of public fora, "the 'traditional public forum,' the 'limited' or 'designated' public forum, the 'nonpublic forum,' and private property." These distinct fora are differentiated by the different obligations the state holds toward the practice of free speech within the fora. The "traditional public forum," made up of public streets, sidewalks, and parks is the most free of these, where the state is forbidden from regulating speech based on content, and only permitted to regulated the "time, place, and manner" of speech acts.[8] "Private property" is the most restrictive, wherein the owner of the property has extensive license to regulate speech as it occurs on her property.[9] *The electrohippies'* action can be

---

[ii]In particular, the work of McPhail, Schweingruber, and McCarthy in "Policing Protests in the United States: 1960-1995," and by Timothy Zick in *Speech Out of Doors* has influenced my thinking in this section.

seen as an attempt to assert a fundamental view of the internet as a "public forum" in the face of its attempted designation as "private property."[10] This assertion comes, by design, into direct confrontation with the WTO's attempt to establish and occupy private and ideologically controlled spaces on the internet, in addition to its function as a force for corporate globalization. This struggle for the definition of online space mirrored the struggle on the streets of Seattle, where protesters clashed with police in an attempted assertion of "public space," and where the anarchistic Black Bloc engaged with physical, spatial representations of globalized corporate capitalism in an attempt to forcefully interpolate the "public space" into the "private space."

The strict physical-world parallelism sought by digitally enabled activists such as the EDT and *the electrohippies* necessitates a physicalized view of the internet itself: the internet itself must be seen as a physical place, albeit one with special attributes. Websites become representative static containers, which maintain an occupying presence on the network even as their content and functionality is pushed off-line by the force of the DDoS. That presence remains in the nonresponsive yet still labeled and branded blankness of the downed website. Conspicuous in its lack of expected messaging and voice, this "presence" is still very much an occupying, informatic structure online. A direct action DDoS seeks to strip away the attractive, humanized facade to reveal a corporate target's reality as black boxed and monolithic, fundamentally unresponsive (metaphorically and actually) to human concerns. This is a paraphrase of the goals of street-level direct action, which seeks to lay bare the true nature of things through unvarnished confrontation with state and corporate structures of power.

As discussed in the first chapter, the signal disruption caused by the activist DDoS can constitute a unit of meaning in and of itself, despite its lack of overt "content." It is a contribution to the larger spectacle of alterity being produced by the acts of direct action. The responsive-made-unresponsive, the available-made-unavailable. The actions themselves produce the reality of alternatives, which are then incorporated into the ensuing media coverage, statements of corporate spokespeople, and reactions of law enforcement, including those present at the scene. As the public consumes the spectacle of destruction/disruption, the manifestation of alternatives, and responses to it, the hope is that they will be drawn out of passive consumption and into action.

Direct action DDoS actions also emphasize the value of "place" in online activism. Some critics of direct action acts of digital activism, such as DDoS actions or website defacements, ask why the activist actions can't be moved off-site, perhaps to a reserved "activist domain," where they would not be so disruptive. This is similar to the "demonstration zones" and "free speech zones" often set up around political party conventions or meetings of international governmental organizations, like the WTO or the G8. In 2004, a federal judge described one such "demonstration zone" to be used at the Democratic National Convention in Boston as a "symbolic affront to the First Amendment."[11] There is critical value in being physically or conceptually proximate to locations that are symbolic of or central to a specific activist cause. Timothy Zick calls these "contested places," which serve to "facilitate, amplify, and convey particular messages."[12] In addition to adding symbolic value to an activist action, contested places offer access to specific audiences who are often connected to the activists' message.[13] Sequestering physical-world activists in an isolated "demonstration zone" or digital activists in a perhaps even more isolated "activist domain" severely hampers their ability to get their message out to individuals to whom it would be the most relevant. The open airing, reception, and discussion of dissenting views are a vital part of democracy. To deny activists access to contested places because of their potential for disruption cripples the public debate. Direct action DDoS aims to engage through temporary disruption, a goal which would be impossible if they were not allowed some access to the contested place of a specific website.

Shouting down your opponent:
The censorship critique

The direct action DDoS, focused on interrupting a given signal stream, is vulnerable to the critique of censorship. This criticism has been most aggressively voiced by hacktivist groups such as Cult of the Dead Cow and Hacktivismo. Jordan and Taylor classified this as the "digitally correct" view, wherein the integrity of the network and the right of individuals to an unfettered flow of information take precedence over the political ideals of activism and civil disobedience present in activist DDoS actions.[14] Hacktivists considered the primary goal of hacktivsm, or technologically based activism, to be defeating state censorship and the disruption of online communications via the creation and distribution of tools to evade censorious regimes.[15] Writing in response to various *electrohippies* DDoS actions, Oxblood Ruffin, a prominent member of the Cult of the Dead Cow, wrote, "No rationale, even in the service of the highest ideals, makes [DDoS actions] anything other than what they are—illegal, unethical, and uncivil. One does not make a better point in a public forum by shouting down one's opponent."[16]

This criticism highlights a difference between hacktivist groups, made up of hackers who became politically active through writing and distributing code and tools beginning in the 1990s,[17] and digitally empowered activists like the EDT and *the electrohippies*, who were more often than not experienced activists who subsequently began using internet tools and capabilities to supplement more traditional, physical-world actions.[18] Hacktivists, coming from a culture that values personal autonomy and the freedom of information,[19] are often strongly opposed to the use of DDoS, viewing it as an abridgment of free speech. Operating mostly in an environment made up of digital code and bits, the acceptance of the silencing of bits as a reasonable tactic of dissent was, and remains, unpalatable to most "old-school" hacktivists.[20]

Ruffin was very clear that he did not consider digitally empowered activist groups like *the electrohippies* to be operating at the same level or with the same clarity of logic as his group: "One does not become a hacktivist merely by inserting an 'h' in front of the word activist or by looking backward to paradigm associated with industrial organization."[21] And it is true, these groups were not operating along the same lines of philosophy and practice. Groups such as Cult of the Dead Cow and, later, Hacktivismo were often engaged in building tools of dubious legality, tools that enabled users to encrypt their communications, evade firewalls and censors, and mask their internet traffic.[22] As a result, the security of the project was paramount. Groups tended to be small and secretive, with definite members rather than a large amorphous pool of participants. In many jurisdictions, the tools that these groups were developing were illegal, and using them exposed the user to legal and sometimes physical risks. It was vital that developers be experienced, skilled coders, and the ranks of serious hacktivists were closed until one could show he or she had the necessary skills.[23] Interestingly, these groups operated in a fashion that more closely resembled what the CAE, the primogenitor to the EDT, had envisioned as the operating model for ECD than how the EDT operated. The CAE envisioned practitioners of "electronic civil disobedience" operating as small, semiautonomous cells of specialized practitioners, each performing a specific action or role within a larger organization while simultaneously maintaining individual identities within the larger group.[24]

The EDT and *the electrohippies* were proponents of legitimacy through mass action. Physical-world parallels were central to their philosophy of practice in the online space. Meaning and vitality was drawn from the simultaneous presence and action of thousands of people, not necessarily any actual or extended effect that action may have on the targeted site. In this sense, it was relatively unimportant to groups like the EDT whether a given action was "successful," that is, whether it brought down a site. Stefan Wray notes that

FloodNet, the DDoS tool designed and used by the EDT in the 1990s and early 2000s, rarely resulted in actual downtime for the targeted sites, and as such, its value lay mostly in the "symbolic gesture" of the "simulated threat."[25] The number of participants and the amount of media coverage the action attracted were most relevant to a judgment of "success" or "failure."

The censorship criticism of activist DDoS actions is sometimes valid, as when the tactic is used against organizations that operate primarily online, such as stand-alone blogs, file-sharing sites, or ISPs, such as the IGC/*Euskal Herria Journal* case, which is explored in the next section. In other instances, the criticism fails to recognize unequal power dynamics between targets and activists, such as when a group of individual activists DDoSes a multinational corporation, the presence of alternative outlets of communication, or the intrinsic value of the DDoSed website to the target. The criticism in many cases also fails to interrogate how censorship could be practiced, if at all, by entities not occupying a dominant position in the current power hierarchy. Drawing an equivalency between the actions of private, nonstate actors and censorship, traditionally conceived of as a state-mediated action or at least an action performed by the more powerful party in a conflict, opens up questions about what entities are capable of performing censorship, particularly in the online space. While DDoS is undoubtedly a "disruptive" tactic,[26] disruption does not always equal a denial of speech rights. For example, in the WTO action described earlier in this chapter, though the central website was disrupted, the abilities of the delegates and the WTO as an organization to communicate their particular agenda to the greater public was not stymied. That the website was slowed down or made more difficult to access did not stop the conference from taking place or prevent the press from covering it. Though certain aspects of the WTO's telecommunications infrastructure were negatively effected, the activists engaged in the DDoS and e-mailing bombing actions cannot be said to be "censoring" the speech of the

WTO. Later in this chapter we will examine a case in which, again, while certain aspects of an organization's data presence were disrupted, their ability to engage in public speech was not disrupted, causing the censorship conception to fall flat.

As has been documented by Ethan Zuckerman and others, there are many nonactivist DDoS actions that do readily fit the state-actor censorship model. Zuckerman catalogued instances where independent media and human rights sites were targeted by government actors with the goal of driving those sites off-line entirely. Due to the high cost of defending against large scale DDoS actions, and the propensity for ISPs in certain jurisdictions to view independent media and human rights sites as potential liabilities, these smaller sites can sometimes be driven off-line completely by a DDoS of relatively short duration.[27] State-sponsored or state-directed DDoS actions are not considered to be activist actions in this analysis, and a DDoS waged to effect the permanent removal of content is not considered to be a proper use of the tactic.

An analysis of extant power dynamics between the organizers, participants, and targets of activist DDoS actions can help address concerns of bullying or censorship that can arise regarding the use of the tactic. As the internet lowers barriers to individual connections across a variety of physical-world borders and barriers, it also enables activism to occur at scales of distance previously unheard of, fostering interactions between individuals and entities that may have been previously impossible, such as allowing individuals to enter into direct confrontation with the fully realized entity of a corporation or state.

Several activist DDoS actions have occurred over international borders, where activists from one country targeted the government websites of another country. An early example of this is the 1995 Strano Netstrike, which was organized by activists in Italy, but targeted the web presence of the French government in order to protest that government's policies. Similarly, the EDT's Zapatista actions were organized in the United States, but targeted the websites of the Mexican president Ernesto Zedillo, and the Frankfurt Stock Exchange, among others, in order to protest the Mexican government's treatment of the Zapatistas. In addition, participants may be drawn from a grab bag of countries and jurisdictions. This practice of "transnational activism"[28] has transformed traditional understandings of state/activist relations.

In these cases, there are several different dynamics to be picked apart. The initial, assumed power struggle between activists and state entities is complicated when those activists are not citizens of the targeted states. The interaction raises questions as to a given state's responsibility for the concerns of foreign civilians and to the global activist public. There is the added power relationship between the state(s) from which the organizers and the bulk of the DDoS action originates and the targeted state. This is a particularly important consideration when allegations of cyberwar are or could be at play. Given the current uncertainty regarding the rules of engagement in international conflicts, organizers engaging in transnational activist actions should take care that they do not inadvertently set off an international incident.

Beyond transnational activism, DDoS actions expand potential modes of interaction between individuals or groups of individuals, and corporations. An important consideration for actions targeting corporate entities is the potential for unintended, adverse effects on the public. As more companies move primary aspects of their public-facing business online, it is important to consider the importance of constant uptime to users for reasons beyond convenience. For example, a temporary disruption in the online presence of a retail service or professional association could be substantially different in scope and effect from a disruption in medical or financial services. Disruption is a highly valuable tool of activism, drawing attention via the spectacle of novelty to issues activists want to highlight. However, in planning actions that aim to disrupt essential services in the medical, financial, or utility spheres, organizers should take into account the potential for unintended damage caused by disruptions in these services.

The *Euskal Herria Journal* and the IGC

Oxblood Ruffin's accusation that DDoS actions are nothing more than "illegal, unethical, and uncivil"[29] censorship is correct when the goal of a DDoS action is to permanently render inaccessible speech on the internet that has no other outlet. One such example is the popular DDoS action launched in Spain against the internet service provider IGC in 1997. The stated goal of the action, initiated and led by persons at this point unknown to this author, was to force IGC to stop hosting the Basque publication *Euskal Herria Journal*.[30] The campaign included network level actions and an e-mail campaign, eventually rendering inaccessible the websites and e-mail of IGC's over 13,000 subscribers. This was a populist-minded action; at one point, the major Spanish newspaper *El Pais* threw its support behind the e-mail bombing campaign and published target e-mail addresses for the IGC, though it later retracted its support and removed the addresses from its website.[31] In the interest of continuing to provide service to its other subscribers, many of which were also minority political publications, IGC was forced to stop hosting *Euskal Herria Journal*, though it did so under protest.[32]

As an ISP, IGC exists primarily, if not entirely, online. Removing IGC's ability to be present online removes its raison d'être and its ability to function as a corporation. A DDoS action against IGC strikes a blow to the core of the organization directly. The stress placed on the IGC network crippled the entire IGC apparatus. System outages affected more than just the *Euskal Herria Journal*'s site, and the e-mail bombing campaign hampered the communications of all who used the IGC's mailservers. The levels of collateral damage at the level of basic communications were high.[33]

The goal of the action against IGC was to force the removal of the *Euskal Herria Journal* website from its servers and by doing so deny *Euskal Herria Journal* access to its *only* outlet for speech. This was an objection to content being available on the internet. For as long as it was successfully running, the DDoS action rendered that content unavailable. The goal of the DDoS action, and the surrounding campaign was the permanent imposition of its immediate effects.

The "Deportation class" action

Not all disruptions of content are equivalent to the silencing of speech, however. This is particularly true when the intent of an action is to change something not wholly present on the internet, such as the behavior of a large, multinational corporation. Here I would like to offer a contrasting example to the Euskal Herria/IGC case. In 2001, two German activist organizations, Kein Mensch ist illegal (No man is illegal) and Libertad! launched the "Deportation Class" action against Lufthansa airlines. This was a coordinated, multipronged protest against the German government's use of the airlines' flights to deport immigrants. Using an adapted version of the EDT's FloodNet tool, some 13,000 people participated in a DDoS action against the airline's homepage, which did experience some downtime over the course of the action.[34] Shortly after the action, which included press releases and physical-world actions at stockholder meetings, Lufthansa stopped allowing the German government to use its flights to deport immigrants.

The Deportation Class action targeted the website of a major airline. While the site itself was rendered briefly inaccessible, the actual corporation, its ability to fly planes, maintain normal operations, and communicate internally and with the media remained for practical purposes unaffected. Unlike the IGC action, which effectively prevented the basic functions of business for the organization, this action neither sought nor achieved a fatal disruption in either the airline's normal operations or modes of communicating internally or externally. This type of action, which only affects the homepage of an organization that does not primarily exist online, has been described as "[tearing] down a poster hung up by the CIA,"[35] with the implication that the action is technologically simplistic and has little practical impact on the organization targeted. It is a symbolic action, performed for the benefit of those participating and those watching.

The stated goal of the Lufthansa action was to disrupt ticket sales, draw public attention to a specific aspect of the airline's business model, and through the focused attention change the corporation's behavior. Though the DDoS action took place on the internet, the effect it sought was not limited, was not even present in the online space. In and of itself, this DDoS action could not have achieved what the EDT set out to accomplish. It took positive behavior on the part of Lufthansa for the "Deportation class" action to achieve its goals, as opposed to the IGC action, which was designed to accomplish its intended effect by the force of the DDoS itself.

Direct action is an ideological mode of activism that encourages activists to disrupt harmful processes and systems at the same time as they attempt to provoke a dramatic, illustrative reaction from their target. It doesn't force activists to channel their dissent through ombudsmen or PR departments, or to curtail their political behavior to that recognized by their targets as "valid." Protesters aren't required to tacitly supply their consent before being permitted to express their dissent. Direct action DDoSes aim to disrupt the functioning of a harmful system or process and provoke a performative reaction and attract attention. These actions give us a lens with which to draw a sharp focus on the importance of relative place in online activism, and to address those critics who would tar all activist DDoS actions with the brush of censorship.

Though all DDoS actions, if they are technologically successful, disrupt computer processes, that is not always their primary goal as political activities. The next chapter will look at those DDoS actions that valued marshaling the attention of the media and the public over any actual services that were interrupted.

Notes

1 ehippies@tesco.net, message posted to diggers350 yahoo group. "WTO Sit-in open!—enter the virtual protest now!" November 29, 1999. Archived at groups.yahoo.com/group/Diggers350/ message/236. Last accessed on February 25, 2014.

2 ehippies@tesco.net, email message from *the electrohippies*. "THE WTO SIT-IN: PHASE 2 STARTS NOW!" December 2, 1999. Message released by *the electrohippies*. Archived at www.thing.net/~rdom/ecd/phasetwo.html. Last accessed on February 25, 2014.

3 Critical Art Ensemble, *Electronic Civil Disobedience and Other Unpopular Ideas* (Brooklyn, NY: Autonomedia, 1996), 10–11.

4 Critical Art Ensemble, *Electronic Civil Disobedience and Other Unpopular Ideas,* 18.

5 A. K. Thompson, *Black Bloc, White Riot: Antiglobalization and the Genealogy of Dissent* (Oakland, CA: AK Press, 2010), 59–80.

6 Laura Portwood-Stacer, *Lifestyle Politics and Radical Activism* (New York, NY: Bloomsbury Academic, 2013), 19.

7 Tim Jordan and Paul A. Taylor, *Hacktivism and Cyberwar: Rebels with a Cause* (New York, NY: Routledge, 2004), 167.

8 Timothy Zick, *Speech Out of Doors: Preserving First Amendment Liberties in Public Places* (Cambridge: Cambridge University Press, 2009), 7.

9 Clark McPhail, David Schweingruber, and John McCarthy, "Policing Protest in the United States: 1960–1995," in *Policing Protest,* edited by Donatella della Porta, and Herbert Reiter (Minneapolis, MN: University of Minnesota Press, 1998), 49–69.

10 McPhail, Schweingruber, and McCarthy, "Policing Protest," 49–69.

11 Zick, *Speech Out of Doors*, 230.

12 Ibid., 105.

13 Ibid., 231.

14 Jordan and Taylor, *Hacktivism and Cyberwar*, 114.

15 Ibid., 90; Rita Raley, *Tactical Media* (Minneapolis, MN: University of Minnesota Press, 2009), 41

16 Oxblood Ruffin, "Hacktivismo," (July 17, 2000), *Cult of the Dead Cow Blog*. Retrieved from http://w3.cultdeadcow.com/cms/2000/07/hacktivismo.html. Last accessed February 25, 2014.

17 Oxblood Ruffin, "cDc, show and prove," Paper presented at the Yale Law School Cybercrime and Digital Law Enforcement Conference (New Haven, CT: March, 2004). Retrieved from http://www.cultdeadcow.com/cDc_files/cDc-0384.html. Last accessed February 2014.

18 Ricardo Dominguez, "Electronic civil disobedience: Inventing the future of online agitprop theater," *Proceedings of the Modern Language Association of America: Theories and Methodologies* 124 (2009): 1806–12.

19 Stefan Wray, "Electronic civil disobedience and the World Wide Web of hacktivism: A mapping of extraparliamentarian direct action net politics," *Switch* 4 (1998). Retrieved from http://switch.sjsu.edu/web/v4n2/stefan/. Last accessed February 25, 2014.

20 Wray, "Electronic civil disobedience and the World Wide Web of Hacktivism."

21 Ruffin, "Hacktivismo."

22 Ruffin, "cDc: show and prove."

23 Ibid.

24 Critical Art Ensemble, *Electronic Civil Disobedience*, 23.

25 Wray, "Electronic civil disobedience and the World Wide Web of Hacktivism."

26 Sasha Costanza-Chock, (2003). "Mapping the repertoire of electronic contention," in *Representing resistance: Media, civil disobedience and the global justice movement,* edited by Andrew Opel and Donnalyn Pompper (Greenwood, NJ: Praeger, 2003), 173–91.

27 Ethan Zuckerman, Hal Roberts, Ryan McGrady, Jillian York, and John Palfrey, *2010 Report on Distributed Denial of Service (DDoS) Attacks* (Berkman Center for Internet and Society Research Publication No. 2010–16) (Cambridge, MA: Berkman Center for Internet and Society, 2010).

28 Sidney Tarrow, *The New Transnational Activism* (Cambridge: Cambridge University Press, 2005).

29 Ruffin, "Hacktivismo."

30 Chris Nicol, "Internet censorship case study: *Euskal Herria Journal*," Melville, South Africa: Association for Progressive Communications. Last accessed February 25, 2014. Retrieved from http://europe.rights.apc.org/cases/ehj.html.

31 Francisco Gor, "Internet y ETA," *El Pais*, September 14, 1997. Last accessed February 25, 2014, http://elpais.com/diario/1997/09/14/opinion/874188011_850215.html.

32 Institute for Global Communications, "Statement on the suspension of the Euskal Herria Journal website." July 18, 1997. Last accessed February 25, 2014. Originally published at http:http://www.igc.org/ehj/. Retrieved from http://www.elmundo.es/navegante/97/julio/18/igc-ehj-en.html.

33 Institute for Global Communications, "Statement on the suspension of the EKJ website."

34 Dominguez, "Electronic Civil Disobedience," 1809.

35 Randall Munroe, "CIA," *XKCD*, August 1, 2011. Last accessed February 25, 2014. Retrieved from http://xkcd.com/932/.

CHAPTER THREE

Which way to the #press channel? DDoS as media manipulation

The direct action DDoS provides participants with the theoretical structure and the tactical pathways to directly interact with systems of oppression. But, though disruption may be an effect of a DDoS action, the disruption itself is not always the greater goal of activists. Often, the disruption caused by the DDoS action is used as a tool to direct and manipulate media attention to issues the activists care about. We saw a related example of this in the Lufthansa/Deportation Class Action covered in the last chapter. The challenge for these types of actions, as with public, performative activism on the street, is getting the media to cover the issues that are driving the activist actions, and not merely the spectacle of the activism itself.

In a campaign that primarily seeks to achieve change through the medium of popular attention, activists must enter into an often uneasy symbiotic relationship with the mass media industry. News coverage of an action may result in further coverage of an organization and a cause, which may, in turn, inform a public outcry or directly influence decision makers to initiate desired change. But, as argued by Todd Gitlin, for a given protest action to attract sympathetic media attention, it must look like what the media expects a protest action to look like: ". . . [protests] become 'newsworthy' only by submitting to the implicit rules of newsmaking (themselves embedded in history) of what a 'story' is, what an 'event' is, what a 'protest' is."[1] The use of innovative tactics and settings presents a challenge as multiple parties (activists, law enforcement, state actors, corporations) attempt to seize the opportunity created by novelty to control the narrative, and define a given action (and subsequent use of the tactic) as legitimate or illegitimate. If a tactic such as DDoS is seen as illegitimate, the media could fail to recognize a given action as "activism" and cover only the novelty, spectacle, and criminality of the tactic being deployed.

This chapter covers some examples of how different DDoS actions and the activists involved with them have interacted with the media. Some were more successful than others. For example, Anonymous is particularly adept at attracting and manipulating the media coverage surrounding its raids, whereas earlier groups like the EDT quickly lost control of the narrative. This chapter also addresses some criticisms specifically directed at media-oriented DDoS actions, including the CAE's principle critique that such acts of "symbolic protest" were, in the online space, fundamentally ineffectual.

Terrorist, hacker, artist, nuisance: The many media reflections of the EDT

One of the first groups to attempt to use DDoS actions as a tool of mass activism was the EDT. Beginning in the late 1990s, the EDT launched a series of "digital storms" supporting the Zapatista struggle in Mexico.[2] The EDT was a quartet of artist-activists, Stefan Wray, Ricardo Dominguez, Carmin Karasic, and Brett Stalbaum. Because of differences in how they believed activism should be practiced online, the four had spun off from an earlier group, the CAE.

Stalbaum and Dominguez developed the tool used to facilitate their DDoS-based actions, a web-based tool called FloodNet. The EDT referred to their actions as "virtual sit-ins," a strategy repeated by subsequent groups such as *the electrohippies*, relying on the historically loaded nature of the term to act as a type of pedagogical shorthand as to the legitimacy and certain formal aspects of the DDoS tactic.[3] They promoted a conceptualization of DDoS as an auxiliary political act, embedded within larger campaigns. While a group using DDoS as a tool of direct action would privilege downtime as a marker of a successful action, this was relatively unimportant to the EDT. Stefan Wray notes that FloodNet, the primary DDoS tool used by the EDT in the 1990s and early 2000s, rarely resulted in actual downtime for the targeted sites.[4] The EDT saw the media attention paid to its actions as a primary goal, taking care to distribute press releases to major media outlets and to announce all actions publicly beforehand.[5]

The EDT did attract news coverage over its active years; however, this coverage did not always cover the deeper political and social issues the group had hoped to draw attention to with their activism. Some articles focused on the spectacle of the EDT and their "virtual sit-ins" in digital culture trend pieces, more interested in performing a roll call of the activist space than in interrogating the motivations and logics behind a specific action. An October 1998 *New York Times* article, headlined "'Hacktivists' of All Persuasions Take Their Struggle to the Web," called the EDT's use of DDoS ". . . computer hacking, so far largely nuisance attacks and the equivalent of electronic graffiti. . . ."[6] Some 14 other individuals and organizations, consistently referred to as "hackers," are mentioned in the 2,025-word article. Stories in the *Ottawa Citizen*,[7] *Computerworld*,[8] and the *Sydney Morning Herald*[9] followed a similar pattern. Other articles grouped the EDT and other activist organizations under the label "cyber-terrorists"[10] or forced their activities into a cyberwar framework, using phrases such as "targeted cyber attacks" and "firing the first shots in a cyber war" to describe protest actions.[11] A June 1999

Christian Science Monitor article quotes a RAND researcher, the director of a social-justice group, and a University of Texas professor as saying that the use of DDoS by the EDT is "idiotic," "not constructive," "not good Internet etiquette," "divisive," and that "the kind of actions espoused by the EDT have been widely shunned by social activists of all stripes."[12] A second *Christian Science Monitor* article, published in July 1999, places the EDT's Zapatista actions exclusively in the company of highly colorful hypotheticals about the dangers of cyberterrorism, while declining to interview any members of the EDT.[13] In 2002, the *Buffalo News* ran a 1,625-word feature article, "Hackers Use Computer Skills to Promote Politically Motivated Mischief, Mayhem," which did not interview any activists, though it did interview multiple academics and computer security researchers. The EDT and *the electrohippies* were grouped together indiscriminately with organizations with significantly different tactics and motivations, such as website defacement and malware distribution, and included theoretical future attacks on infrastructure. All groups, real and imaginary, were referred to as "hackers" or "hacktivists."[14]

While the "cyber-terrorist" label and characterizations of the EDT's activist actions as "attacks" or acts of "cyber war" are clearly prejudicial, it is worth taking a moment or two to unpack how the "hacker" characterization also operates as a prejudicial description, one which has the effect of depoliticizing activist actions and fostering perceptions of such actions as criminal and transgressive. The media's use of the stereotypical hacker figure to promote a social fear of technology and pervasive environment of technoparanoia is deep and complex, and there is not enough space to fully explore it here, but I will attempt a brief sketch. By the late 1990s and early 2000s, the media tropes for the coverage of computer matters had begun to solidify. The word "hacker" was, and is still now, used by the news media as a catchall term to apply to any type of criminal or "bad" computer activity, including those that did not break any laws. The hacker figure himself (media depictions of male hackers outnumber those of female hackers by a wide margin) became a type of "folk devil," a personification of our anxieties about technology, the technologically mediated society, and our increasingly technologically mediated selves. The hacker, as depicted in film and on the 6 o'clock news, is the central deviant of the information society.[15]

The hacker-as-folk-devil figure has several persistent characteristics. He stands separate from "normal" society; his life is socially, economically, and often physically isolated. See, for example, the stereotypic image of the adolescent hacker living in his parents' basement. Because he is socially alienated, he lacks the normal social checks on his behavior, and is instead engaged in compulsive, competitive cycles with other hackers, who egg on each other's antisocial behavior. He doesn't abide by conventional morality because he is immature or young, and self-importantly believes the rules don't apply to him. His relationship with technology is pathological, and he is sometimes described as being "addicted" to computers or the internet. His abilities are often depicted as far surpassing those of the average person. Paul Ohm described this aspect of the hacker folk devil as the Superuser, someone whose technological skills are so advanced as to be seen as essentially magical to most observers.[16] The hacker is locationless and decentralized, able to cause harm far from his actual location. The hacker folk devil is therefore cast as abnormal, alienated from conventional socials morals, a predictably bad actor, capable and willing to cause great harm to individuals, corporations, and the state. Not only is the hacker tarred with this brush, but anyone who participates in activities or holds views associated with hackers are held guilty by association. In tagging the EDT as "hackers," these news articles characterize digital activists and their activities as antisocial, essentially nonpolitical, and potentially dangerous to the public at large.[17]

The EDT conceived of their FloodNet-powered DDoS actions in the late 1998 and 1999 primarily as media events, meant to direct popular attention to the Zapatista struggle. However, as Graham Meikle argues, because much of the news coverage was either reactionary early-cyberwar rhetoric or facilely focused on FloodNet's novelty, it would be a stretch to consider the FloodNet actions to be successful on that level.[18] Many of the articles covering the EDT can be seen as attempts on the part of the news media to categorize the activists and their actions into some sort of known quantity, terrorists or hackers or artists. The novelty of the DDoS tactic provided this sorting opportunity, but the coverage did not go so far as to cover the actual story of the politics behind the tactic's use.

The EDT's problems with myopic press coverage highlight the difficulties activists face when attempting to tie their messaging strongly to their disruptive action. The "digital" or "virtual" sit-in nomenclature used by the EDT and other groups is highly evocative, allowing activists to build off the pedagogical and cultural capital of historical physical-world sit-ins.[19] However, the metaphor glosses over many challenges inherent to the digital form, particularly that of proximity to messaging. In a physical-world sit-in, the rhetorical proximity of the protest to the target is central to the disruption. Though this has sometimes been challenged in the United States with the establishment of "protest zones" in locations deemed to be sensitive, the physical closeness of protest actions to direct or symbolic targets is a valuable part of activist messaging, as discussed earlier.

This type of proximal messaging is not natural in the online space. DDoS actions in particular may by invisible to the public. A user attempting to access a targeted site may have no exposure to the protest's messaging at all and may not even register that an action is taking place. All that is apparent to them is that the site they are looking for is operating poorly or not at all. Not only does this represent a failed opportunity for the campaign, but it also shifts blame/credit to the target. Without effective messaging, a given campaign may appear to be incoherent disruption, giving the press an excuse to probe no deeper than chaotic first impressions. We will now move on to some other examples of DDoS campaigns that fared differently in the media sphere than the EDT did.

Allies in the toywar

In December 1999, the EDT, the Swiss art group etoy, and culture jamming group ®™mark (pronounced art-mark) launched "The Twelve Days of Christmas" action using the EDT's FloodNet DDoS tool. Their target was the retail site eToys.com, which had filed a lawsuit against the etoy group over the ownership of the URL etoy.com.[20] As part of the greater "toywar" campaign, which involved physical-world demonstrations, publicity and letter writing campaigns, and a multiplayer online game, the "12 Days of Christmas" DDoS campaign was intended, according to Ricardo Dominguez, to ". . . represent the presence of a global group of people gathered to bear witness to a wrong,"[21] and to disrupt eToys.com's online operations during the critical Christmas shopping season. Some 1,700 individuals participated in the DDoS action. In January 2000, eToys.com dropped its suit and paid the court costs of etoy.

The toywar campaign enjoyed significant coverage in the mainstream news media, mostly due to the ongoing legal drama of the eToys.com lawsuit. The case was seen as a test of the lengths corporations could go to police their trademark online, and was followed closely by the US business press. As the case played out, inside and outside the courtroom, multiple stories appeared in *Wired*, the *New York Times*, the *Washington Post*, the *Guardian*, *USA TODAY*, and other international news outlets. Unlike coverage of the EDT and *the electrohippies*, the toywar coverage, with few exceptions, did not focus on the technical machinations of the protest action or attempt to classify ®™mark, etoy, or the EDT as terrorists, criminal hackers, or even cybersquatters. Rather, news outlets made extensive use of the David and Goliath narrative to describe what was seen as a legal dispute between a large corporate online retailer and a small avant-garde art group.

Of particular interest here is the emergence of vocal third parties advocating for etoy. In coverage of the EDT and *the electrohippies*, any third parties quoted who were not also digital activists or hacktivists were predominantly information security professionals or others who condemned the concept of electronic civil disobedience in general. The etoy/toywar coverage, on the other hand, included the voices of John Perry Barlow, attorneys at the Electronic Frontier Foundation, and luminaries from the tech art world, all of whom supported etoy. *Wired*'s 1999 article, "Be Grateful for Etoy," quotes John Perry Barlow extensively, as he calls the etoy/eToys fight "the battle of Bull Run," and invokes the ghost of internet luminary Jon Postel, saying "If Jon Postel were alive, he'd be in tears." The article goes on to quote EFF legal director Shari Steele as saying "Shame on eToys for misusing the law in this way," and characterizing the case as a "clear-cut case of a business bullying a group of artists. . . ."[22] Also in 1999, an article published in the *Washington Post* quotes Karin Spaink, a judge for the 1996 Prix Arts Electronica, which has been awarded to etoy, criticizing the scope of a judicial decision in the case which restricted the ability of etoy to sell "stock" in the United States.[23]

The presence of the solid, easily understood narrative structure of the court case allowed the news media to focus on the nuances of the dispute and the accompanying "12 Days of Christmas" DDoS action. As a result the coverage was much more sympathetic to both etoy's legal claim and the legitimacy of the DDoS action and contained a wider range of voices than coverage of other EDT or *electrohippies'* actions.

Anonymous and the media: Manipulation, entertainment, and readymades

Anonymous, a loose collection of internet denizens that sprang from the unmoderated image board 4chan, has, over the past few years, rapidly increased their capacity to attract and manipulate mainstream media attention.[24] This ability was on display during the Operation PayBack DDoS campaign in December 2010, also known as Operation Avenge Assange. During this action, the high level of quotable, embed-able graphic and video artifacts produced by the group allowed them a level of control over the media narrative that, for example, the EDT had never enjoyed. Anonymous is, as a group, difficult for the media to cover, but their cultural artifacts are highly accessible online. By pushing the peer production and distribution of these artifacts, which include video manifestos, graphical calls to action, and solidarity images, Anonymous was able, to a certain extent, dictate the visual tools and language used in the media's coverage of Operation Payback.

Operation PayBack was a series of DDoS actions against a variety of entities that Anonymous perceived as taking hostile action toward Wikileaks. Primarily using the LOIC tool (which will be examined in detail in Chapter 6), Anonymous targeted more than ten different sites over the course of 4 days, from December 6 through December 10, 2010, including those of the Swedish Prosecution Authority, EveryDNS, senator Joseph Lieberman, MasterCard, two Swedish politicians, Visa, PayPal, and Amazon.com.[25] Many of the sites targeted experienced at least some amount of downtime.

Unlike the EDT, *the electrohippies*, and other groups discussed in this book, Anonymous had, in 2010, a reputation, in many ways a purposefully cultivated one, for being extremely effective and unpleasant trolls with unpredictable methods of choosing their targets. The majority of the media coverage of Anonymous and Operation Payback was characterized by an unwillingness to critically assess Anonymous as an activist group or Operation Payback as an activist action and a rampant confusion about the facts. There was genuine fear that any organization or individual could be Anonymous' next target, and very few people were willing to hang a bull's-eye on their back by being publicly critical of them, particularly journalists and news organizations that did not fully understand the technological tactics so freely deployed. Add to this the fact that one of Anonymous' primary methods for spreading information about operations and raids was through the public distribution of slickly produced videos, graphics, and public social media streams, and the result was, in many cases, news organizations embedding Anonymous videos and call-to-action posters directly in news stories. Examples of this could be found in the *Washington Post*[26] and the social media news site *Mashable*.[27] In an article entitled, "'Anonymous' attacks Visa.com, Mastercard.com, in support of WikiLeaks," the *Washington Post* embedded a call-to-action video entitled, "Operation Payback #Anonymous Message RE: ACTA, SOPA, PIPA, Internet Censorship and Copyright," which in turn linked to an Anon-run twitter account. The social networking news site *Mashable,* in a post entitled "Operation Payback Targets Amazon.com," linked to numerous Twitter accounts, which were tweeting scheduling and targeting information, as well as linking to the *Encyclopedia Dramatica* page on the LOIC DDoS tool. They also embedded the same call-to-action video that the *Washington Post* also included in their coverage.

The decentralized, leaderless nature of Anonymous made direct coverage of the group difficult. After all, there were no official spokespeople for the press to rely on, and there was a constant flow of Pastebin statements, videos, and Photoshopped posters popping up in all corners of the internet, all claiming to be from Anonymous. The extreme horizontal nature of Anonymous meant that literally anyone could claim to speak for the group. Anonymous set up a press channel on one of its IRC servers, where members of the press could chat with Anons, but many members of the press were simply not aware of it or lacked the technological skills to access the channel on their own. The combination of the demands of the 24-hour news cycle and an unpredictable, unreliable subject meant that a sizable percentage of the coverage was made up of reprinting Anonymous press releases and posters as journalists scrambled for new material on an almost hourly basis. Often an Anonymous artifact that had been "legitimated" by one news source would quickly find its way into others, expanding dramatically the range of influence for certain artifacts. For example, the *Washington Post* and *Mashable* article cited earlier both embedded the same call-to-action video, which had originally been linked to by the *New York Times* blog, "The Lede." This pattern of news organizations repeating and homogenizing coverage over the course of an ongoing event fits with the pattern described by Pablo Boczkowski and Martin de Santos in their 2007 examination of homogenization in the Argentine print and online news industries. Boczkowski and de Santos found that online news sites were particularly prone to high levels of "content overlap" on fast moving stories that demanded repeated updates throughout the day. Boczkowski and de Santos ascribe this homogeneity of coverage to "not technology per se, manifested in the emergence of a new medium, but technical practices, or how journalists use the technology to make news."[28] Anonymous' continual furnishing of quotable, embeddable, compelling descriptive content exacerbated an already extant system of aggregating from available information feeds to maintain the constant flow of news content.

This explosion of coverage was a boon to Anonymous in terms of participant population. Anons have subsequently claimed that during Operation Payback, the number of participants active in their IRC channels rose from an average of 70 participants to over 7,000.[29] It is likely that without this influx of new participants, the Operation Payback DDoS actions would not have resulted in the downtime they did.[i] This substantial increase in active participants during Operation Payback can be credited in part to the extensive, relatively uncritical media coverage given to the December stage of Operation Payback.

---

[i]As addressed in Chapter 6, the use of illicit, nonvolunteer botnets contributed substantially to achieved downtime.

Shadows in the monitor:
The CAE's symbolic dissent critique

In the 1996 essay, "Electronic Civil Disobedience,"[30] the CAE posited an evolution on the traditional, physical-world model of civil disobedience. As systems of power migrated from the brick-and-mortar infrastructure of physical buildings to reside primarily as data constructs on the internet, the CAE argued, so too must systems of resistance and protest. ECD as conceived of by the CAE sought to translate the philosophies of disruptive protest from the physical world to the networked world via a system of small, semiautonomous cells of specialized practitioners, each performing a specific action or role within a larger organization, while simultaneously maintaining individual identities within the larger group.[31] Central to the CAE's vision was the clandestine and essentially closed nature of the actions, carried out by semiautonomous cells rather than by a large, public, mass demonstration of dissent. The CAE describes this as an "inversion" of traditional civil disobedience.[32] This particular philosophy sprang from a belief that ECD "is an underground activity that should be kept out of the public/popular sphere (as in the hacker tradition) and the eye of the media . . ." because ". . . there is no corporate or government agency that is not fully prepared to do battle in the media."[33] The CAE criticized the actions of groups such as the EDT and others for engaging in public, spectacle-oriented "simulated" actions over "clandestine policy subversion" and direct action.

The CAE felt that the mass-action, media spectacle tactics that the EDT employed, including their use of DDoS actions as attention directors, would ultimately be completely ineffectual at effecting change in corporate and government actors. However, this criticism lifts the tactic out of the context of larger actions or campaigns it might be associated with. The validity of the tactic is equally dependent on the activist structure that surrounds it as any qualities inherent in it.

DDoS actions were not primarily conceived of as stand-alone actions. EDT member Stephen Wray notes that "we are likely to see a proliferation of hybridized actions that involve a multiplicity of tactics, combining actions on the street and actions in cyberspace."[34] To divest DDoS of its "component" nature[35] is to place on its shoulders a weight of ontological justification that no tactic alone could bear.

Similar to the censorship criticism leveled by the hacktivist groups, the CAE's criticism of DDoS as ineffective is as much a description of the different goals and operating philosophies at work between these types of activist organization as it is an autonomous critique.

What does winning look like?

Critics of activist DDoS actions routinely raise the question of measures of success. At a technological level, it is becoming more and more difficult for volunteer-based DDoS action to cause any downtime on major corporate sites. It would be virtually impossible for such an action to crash a modern site without technological augmentation. This is not a new development, even in the early 2000s, the FloodNet powered DDoS actions run by the EDT rarely resulted in downtime.[36] So if an actual denial-of-service caused by server downtime is an unlikely result of an activist DDoS action, what then is an appropriate measure of the success of any given action?

In this, the CAE's criticism of DDoS actions as symbolic and simulated reverses to become its virtue. When used within a broader action to expand opportunities for engagement and participation, DDoS tactics create what Foucault termed a "plurality of resistances," each action being a provocation with not-necessarily-certain desired results.[37] Ricardo Dominguez described this as a "permanent cultural resistance; there is no endgame."[38] The value of this symbolic resistance is not necessarily in its overt effect on the system it ostensibly targets, but rather in its effects on its participants and on the reflective fields that surround it as it occurs, including media and culture. Particularly in its value as a tool of biographical impact, the subject of the next chapter, DDoS acts as a tool for the revelation of "hidden transcripts" of resistance.[39] This is particularly apparent in the case of the Anonymous Operation Payback, wherein the vast majority of the actions and organization took place online among individuals who had not met in the physical world. As a tactic whose strength is in the digitized power of a crowd, the DDoS serves as an open action wherein individual participants "recognize the full extent to which their claims, their dreams, their anger is shared by other subordinates with whom they have not been in direct touch."[40] This is a quality which will become increasingly valuable as digital activism continues to be unbounded by state borders and moves toward a transnational operational norm.

Notes

1   Todd Gitlin, *The Whole World Is Watching* (Berkeley, CA: University of California Press, 2003), 3.

2   Electronic Disturbance Theater, e-mail sent from the Electronic Disturbance Theater, "24 Hour Digital Storm On the Mexican Government. August 26th 1999," sent on August 25, 1999. Archived at http://www.thing.net/~rdom/ecd/storm99.html. Last accessed February 25, 2014.

3   Brett Rolfe, "Building an electronic repertoire of contention," *Social Movement Studies*, 4 (2005): 65–74.

4   Wray, "Electronic civil disobedience and the World Wide Web of Hacktivism."

5   Dominguez, "Electronic Civil Disobedience," 1809.

6   Amy Harmon, "Hacktivists of All Persuasions Take Their Struggle to the Web," *New York Times*, October 31, 1999.

7   Bob Paquin, "E-Guerillas in the Mist," *Ottawa Citizen*, October 26, 1998.

8   Deborah Radcliff, "Meet the 'Hacktivist'," *Computerworld*, October 16, 2000.

9   Maria Nguyen, "Armchair Activism," *Sydney Morning Herald*, August 17, 2002.

10 Tom Regan, "When terrorists turn to the Internet," *Christian Science Monitor*, July 1, 1999; Editorial, "Cyber-terrorism's threat becoming real," *Hamilton Spectator*, November 10, 1999.

11 John Lasker, "Hackers Use Computer Skills to Promote Politically Motivated Mischief, Mayhem," *Buffalo News*, May 14, 2002.

12 Paul Van Slambrouck, "Newest tool for Social Protest: The Internet," *Christian Science Monitor*, June 18, 1999.

13 Regan, "When terrorists turn to the internet."

14 Lasker, "Hackers Use Computer Skills to Promote Politically Motivated Michief, Mayhem."

15 Molly Sauter, "If Hackers Didn't Exist, Governments Would Have to Invent Them," *The Atlantic*, July 5, 2012. Last accessed February 25, 2014. Retrieved from http://www.theatlantic.com/technology/archive/12/07/if-hackers-didnt-exist-governments-would-have-to-invent-them/259463/.

16 Paul Ohm, "The Myth of the Superuser: Fear, Risk, and Harm Online," University of Colorado Law Legal Studies Research Paper No. 07–14, *UC David Law Review* 41 (2008): 1327.

17 Molly Sauter, "Policy Effects of the Media Portrayals of Hacktivists," SXSW Interactive, March 2012. Slides available http://prezi.com/waiqewbhgh5q/hackers-in-the-media-sxsw/. Audio available http://schedule.sxsw.com/2012/events/event_IAP12520/.

18 Graham Meikle, *Future Active* (New York, NY: Routledge, 2002), 155.

19 Rolfe, "Building an electronic repertoire of contention."

20 McKenzie Wark, "Toywars: Conceptual art meets conceptual business," *M/C: A Journal of Media and Culture* 6 (2003). Retrieved from http://journal.media-culture.org.au/0306/02-toywars.php/. Last accessed February 25, 2014.

21 Ricardo Dominguez, quoted in Wark, "Toywars."

22 Steve Kettmann, "Be Grateful for Etoy," *WIRED*, December 17, 1999.

23 Richard Leiby, "Etoys vs Etoy: A Clash of Commerce and Art," *Washington Post*, December 10, 1999.

24 Whitney Phillips, "The house that fox built: Anonymous, spectacle and cycles of amplification," *Television and New Media* 14 (2013): 494–509.

25 Sean-Paul Correll (2010), "'Tis the season of DDoS: WikiLeaks edition," *PandaLabs Blog*, December 15, 2010. Last accessed February 25, 2014, http://pandalabs.pandasecurity.com/tis-the-season-of-DDoS-wikileaks-editio/.

26 Melissa Bell, "Anonymous attacks Visa.com, Mastercard.com in support of WikiLeaks," *The Washington Post*, December 8, 2010. Last accessed Feburary 25, 2014, http://voices.washingtonpost.com/blog-post/2010/12/mastercardcom_hacked_by_wikile.html.

27 Brenna Erlich (2010), "Operation Payback targets Amazon.com," *Mashable.com*, December 9, 2010. Last accessed February 25, 2014, http://mashable.com/2010/12/09/operation-payback-amazo/.

28 Pablo Boczkowski and Martin de Santos, "When More Media Equals Less News: Patterns of Content Homogenization in Argentina's Leading Print and Online Newspapers," *Political Communication* 24 (2007): 167–80.

29 Gabriella Coleman, "Our weirdness is free," *Triple Canopy* 15 (2012). Retrieved from http://canopycanopy.com/15/our_weirdness_is_free/. Last accessed February 25, 2014.

30 Critical Art Ensemble, *Electronic Civil Disobedience*, 7–32.

31 Ibid., 23.

32 Critical Art Ensemble, *Digital Resistance: Explorations in Tactical Media* (Brooklyn, NY: Autonomedia, 2001), 14.

33 Critical Art Ensemble, *Digital Resistance*, 15.

34 Stefan Wray quoted in Raley, *Tactical Media*, 44.

35 Raley, *Tactical Media*, 44.

36 Wray, "Electronic civil disobedience and the World Wide Web of Hacktivism."

37 Michel Foucault, *A History of Sexuality, Volume One: An Introduction* (New York, NY: Vintage, 1990), 185.

38 Ricardo Dominguez quoted in Raley, *Tactical Media*, 46.

39 James Scott, *Domination and the Arts of Resistance: Hidden Transcripts* (New Haven: Yale University Press, 1990).

40 Scott, *Domination and the Arts of Resistance*, 223.

CHAPTER FOUR

Show me what an activist looks like: DDoS as a method of biographical impact

We've looked at direct action and media manipulation through their specific theories of change, models of practice, and historical case studies. Another model for the use of DDoS in activism is as a tool of "biographical impact," or the impact the experience of participation has on the individual activist. Doug McAdam traced biographical impact as it occurred among activists who participated in Freedom Rides during the Civil Rights Movement, measuring to what extent activist participation could predict future political radicalization and involvement. He differentiated between two varieties of biographical impact: conversion and alternation. "Conversion" is defined as "a radical transformation of a person's life, including their self-conception, network of associations and larger worldview ... [which] tends to occur in groups that demand the exclusive loyalties of its members and maintain a hostile stance toward mainstream society."[1] The milder "alternation" consists of "identity changes that are not as drastic as conversion ... which are part of or grow out of existing programs of behavior."[2] Alternation can take place in groups that are "relatively more inclusive and tolerant of the other attachment of its members" but which ". . . can be very demanding of a person's time, energy, and loyalties."[3] The more culturally immersive an activist's experience is, in terms of exposure to like-minded peers, the creation of social and technical structures of support and interaction, and the furnishing of a vocabulary to articulate the experience, the more likely it is to result in alternation or conversion on the part of the individual.

Does participating in a DDoS action make a person more likely to stay politically involved? Could a DDoS action be considered a radicalizing moment for its participants? McAdam's language of biographical impact, conversion, and alternation provide the tools needed to examine what, if any, impact a DDoS action has on the people involved.

Here, it is particularly useful to remember that DDoS is often most effectively used within the context of a larger campaign, wherein multiple tactics are utilized. Ideally, these tactics each reinforce a certain ideological stance of the group and provide opportunities to lead participants from one tactical action to another. In this chapter I argue that Anonymous, because of certain aspects of how its culture functions and perpetuates, is particularly apt to have a strong biographical impact on participants rising to the level of alternation.

The culture of the Hive

The precise nature of Anonymous is a difficult thing to pin down, but it is best described as a "culture."[4] Quinn Norton articulates the characterization of Anonymous-as-culture this way:

> It takes cultures to have albums, idioms, and iconography, and I was swimming in these and more. Anonymous is a nascent and small culture, but one with its own aesthetics and values, art and literature, social norms and ways of production, and even its own dialectic language.[5]

David Auerbach identifies Anonymous with what he calls "A-culture," a set of larger cultural norms and practices that broadly encompass the trolling, anonymous, internet-based subaltern counter public of which Anonymous is a part. A-culture is strongly defined by the online communications technologies on which it was originally reliant. These technologies were text and static-image based, fundamentally anonymous in their attribution structure, and "evanescent," containing no archive of interactions or communications. Core to A-culture, Auerbach observes, are the practices of ironizing, recreational offense, self-documentation, elitism, and heightened meta-awareness, coupled with persistent economies of suspicion and unreality.[6] I would add to this highly democratized modes of appropriation-based production, which, while being extremely social and open, operate as an effective shibboleth into the active culture. Knowledge of and competencies with certain suites of cultural reference are expected of participants. The ability to actively participate in the production of cultural artifacts, using a practice-vocabulary based in the appropriation and remix of images from popular culture and A-culture itself, is also expected.

The evolution of Anonymous from an inward-facing group concerned with its own amusement often at the expense of outsiders to an open activist culture adept at attention-building and attractive to the uninitiated occurred over time, though several trigger events hastened developments significantly. Prior to the WikiLeaks-related actions of 2010, Anonymous was known in part for the internet memes which spilled forth from the board (some examples are rickrolling[i] and lolcats,[ii]) and in part for the intensely personal harassment campaigns and aggressive "raids" it conducted across the internet.[7]

---

[i]"Rickrolling" is a "bait and switch" meme, wherein a person is tricked into clicking on a link leading to Rick Astley's 1987 "Never Gonna Give You Up" music video.

[ii]Lolcats are pictures of cats with humorous text inscribed on them, written in a specific tailored grammar. For more on lolcats, please see the excellent work of Kate Miltner.

Sometimes these raids were DDoS actions; at other times they were site invasions, wherein massive numbers of Anons would converge on a site to monopolize comment threads or occupy locations in massively multiplayer online games.[8] A key factor was the aesthetic of "doing it for the lulz," an agenda of having fun at the expense of another.[9] Like many active in hacker and internet culture, Anons valued free speech and the autonomy of the internet, although their early raids were more often than not focused on showing up their target and generally causing hilarious (to them) chaos.

Beginning in 2008 with Operation Chanology, the actions of Anonymous began to take on a more overtly political tone. Operation Chanology targeted the Church of Scientology, initially for attempting to force the takedown of a video featuring Tom Cruise talking about the church, but the Op's list of grievances later expanded to more general objections to the church itself.[10] The operation involved DDoS actions and other digital tactics as well as physical-world street protests. It marked the first occasion Anonymous raids crossed over into the physical world, with masked Anons gathering outside Scientology Centers in various cities and countries, holding signs and protesting the church's policies. This was a controversial step among Anons. Some objected to taking Anon actions to the streets, arguing that Anonymous should restrict its actions to the online space.[iii] Others felt that the political tone of Operation Chanology was in opposition to the "spirit of the lulz" that had previously defined Anonymous.[11] Operation Chanology represented a shift in the makeup and tenor of Anonymous. The "lulz" lost its purity of purpose, and raids began to represent a developing political sensibility,

---

[iii]Previous to this, the Electronic Disturbance Theater (EDT), *the electrohippies*, etoy, and other groups had used DDoS as a tactic within larger campaigns, often in coordination with other organizations. Anonymous' internal dispute about coupling street protests with DDoS actions and other digital tactics is special to Anonymous, and arose in part because of the "internet-native" nature of the group, which had previously been active only in the online space.

one heavily influenced by internet libertarianism, free-speech absolutism, moderate levels of anarchy,[12] and a strongly held belief in the ethical treatment of cats.[13]

Anonymous' activist incarnation is primarily represented by two visual icons: the Guy Fawkes mask, and an empty black suit. Of these, the Guy Fawkes mask has proven the more durable, and more effective, representation. It is also an efficient metaphor for the identity subsumation that occurs as individuals become involved in Anonymous actions. Anonymous' conception of identity within the culture is at base a pluralistic one. The power and attraction of Anonymous is built out of the concept of the hoard, the mass, the unstoppable wave. "We are legion. We do not forgive. We do not forget. Expect us," is the unofficial motto of Anonymous. It appears in videos, image macros, and all manner of viral media produced by and around Anonymous. The phrase "We are legion" comes from the Gospel of Mark, from the story where Jesus exorcises a demon from a possessed man. When asked for its name, the demon replies, "αὐτῷ Λεγιὼν ὄνομά μοι, ὅτι πολλοί ἐσμεν:" meaning, "I am [called] legion, for we are many." The original phrase, perhaps better than the Anonymous adaptation, captures the peculiar nature of the Anonymous identity meme, wherein many different identities are drawn up and into a single identity. One central source is made more powerful by the participation of many individuals. But those individual identities move in and out of different states of participation. Individuals join in under the banner of Anonymous, temporarily subsuming their personalities under the larger, metapersonality of the Anonymous hoard.[14]

Adding to the collective identity nature of Anonymous is its use of collective pseudonyms or "improper names," as described by Marco Deseriis.[15] Deseriis notes that improper names, as they are extended to and pass among multiple participants, empower individuals by blurring the line between an autonomous actor and the crowd behind her. Such improper names also extend the zone of influence of individuals, as each action taken under the collective pseudonym becomes incorporated into the overarching sense of identity.[16]

A technological parallel for this, which will be examined in detail in Chapter 6, is the "Hive Mind" mode built into a version of the LOIC DDoS tool, which was popular during the Operation Payback DDoS actions. When running in Hive Mind mode, rather than independently targeting and deploying the tool, a participant choreography familiar from the EDT's and *the electrohippies'* use of the FloodNet tool, you could instead place your computer under the control of a central IRC server. By joining this voluntary botnet, you were able to add your individual digital voice to the stream of other voices being controlled by an overarching persona: "I am legion, for we are many."

Three aspects of Anonymous culture and activist practice make it more likely that individuals who participate in the Operation Payback DDoS actions would experience alternation or conversion as a result. First, the communications channels used for planning, publicity, and in-group socializing were often open and public. These included many IRC channels and various social media accounts. Through IRC and social media channels, participants were immersed in a like-minded peer community, one in the throes of an intensely active period whose energy persisted after the end of the Operation Payback actions. Very shortly after the end of Operation Payback, the Arab Spring, the HBGary hack, Occupy Wall Street, a number of high profile hacker arrests, and other events repeatedly triggered and reinforced the activist instincts of the Anonymous population, who continued to use the communications practices used in Operation Payback.

Second, Anonymous visual culture relies on appropriation and remix practices, liberally quoting from pop culture and from itself in persistent, repetitive cycles of production. This means the ability to quickly produce highly relevant cultural products is easily available to members of the in-group, already privy to the layers of meaning and reference contained within the symbols. For outsiders, particularly outsiders in the media, the hieroglyphic nature of Anonymous visual culture, which during Operation Payback and its aftermath was experiencing a super-proliferation online, made the images and videos highly useful for their reductive, symbolic value. The use by the media of these artifacts of Anonymous visual culture to represent Anonymous further reinforced their value as metasymbolic objects within the culture and made their production a more experientially valuable enterprise. As the visual culture spread, the ability to repeatedly produce culturally consistent artifacts became a more important marker of insider status than simply recognizing or correctly interpreting specific cultural tropes.

Third, the "hive" model of action valued by Anonymous activists, which requires a merging of personal agency and identity with an overarching supra-identity structure, assigns all participants the activist identity, regardless of experience or participation level. Even "passive" participants whose favored mode of participation was turning on Hive Mind and walking away could be seen as just as important to the success of the action as those who man their terminals for the duration. Those who had considered themselves to be an audience in the world of politics and industry could become actors, strengthened by the invisible yet palpable presence of thousands of their new comrades-in-arms.

All these factors reinforce one another and channel participants from one impactful activity to the next. An individual may initially encounter a call-to-action on Twitter, participate in a DDoS action, and subsequently contribute to planning chats, collaborative manifesto writing, or video production. Each draws the participant deeper into the culture and creates more opportunities for biographical impact. Participants may also dip into one or two activities, or participate once and never return to the culture. However, the cultural nature of Anonymous actions fosters many opportunities for participation for those who are interested.

Anonymous' hacker identity

Although early practitioners of mass DDoS actions sought to create an overarching collective identity for their actions, it usually extended only to a vaguely defined "witnessing" crowd, similar to how Ricardo Dominguez described the participants in the etoy/toywar DDoS action: ". . . a global group of people gathered to bear witness to a wrong."[17] This is in keeping with the EDT's underlying conceit of DDoS as "virtual sit-in." The internet-based nature of the DDoS releases the participant from the challenges of distance and physical space, but she is still valued as a far-flung, unaffiliated individual. She does not participate because she is culturally obligated, but because the networked nature of the DDoS allows her to add her presence to whatever cause she feels drawn to. A unified, restrictive cultural identity would have undercut the "global" mass action aesthetic sought (but not always achieved) by the organizers, particularly in actions which purposefully crossed national borders, such as the EDT's Zapatista actions or the Strano Netstrikes, a series of DDoS actions in December of 1995 targeting the websites of various French government offices in protest against their nuclear policies. The actions were organized by an Italian group called the Strano Network, led by Tommaso Tozzi.[18] As will be explored in Chapter 6, however, the EDT's reliance on very specific sociopolitical and linguistic frames within their actions, though not an overt cultural identity, served to restrict the global distribution of their actions.

While the EDT and other groups based their political philosophies and group cultures within wide frames of anticapitalist/anticorporate globalization activist culture, Anonymous actions are strongly embedded within the restricted, bounded, cultural frame of A-culture. This allowed participants to immerse themselves in a pervasive activist setting, and added to the biographical impact value of participating in the action. This culture also contains a deeply performative aspect.

Drawing on media tropes of hackers and technology, as well as internet meme culture, Anonymous culture plays with stereotypes to create a public identity that is anarchic, humorous, and trollish, feeding off the fearful or angry reactions of the uninformed. This is generally known as "for the lulz." As explained by Gabriella Coleman:

> Trolling on 4chan often consists of an unpredictable combination of the following: telephone pranking, having many unpaid pizzas sent to the target's home, DDoSing, and most especially, splattering personal information, preferably humiliating, all over the Internet. Since at least 2006, "Anonymous" has conducted many such trolling campaigns. The motivating force and emotional consequence for the instigators of many acts of trolling, including those on 4chan, are cited as the "lulz," a pluralization and bastardization of laugh out loud (lol). Lulz denotes the pleasures of trolling, but the lulz is not exclusive to trolling. The lulz can also refer more generally to lighthearted and amusing jokes, images, and pranks.[19]

The hacker figure featured prominently in news media and film is a type of modern folk devil. Based in apocalyptic techno-paranoia, popular media stokes common fears that armies of basement-dwelling adolescent males are eager to dish out vindictive mayhem to a society so tied to technology (and yet so clueless as to its inner workings) that it would be unable to adequately defend itself. The hacker in this story is a dark, unseen force in the network, decentralized and able to cause havoc far from his physical location. Socially alienated and cut off from normal moral checks, he engages in pathological, compulsive behaviors with other hackers. The characterization of such a pathological cycle of behavior is cited by James Aho as critical to the demonizing of the social enemy, a role the hacker figure occupies in our modern technology-reliant society.[20] The hacker's nights are spent trying to outdo other hackers in technological feats of mayhem and disruption, and his skills are beyond the ken of any "normal" person.[21]

Anonymous has seized delightedly upon this mythological figure, further reveling in epithets attached to them by the news media, such as "Internet Hate Machine," originally coined in a hysterical news segment aired by a FOX affiliate in July of 2007. Their slogan, "We are Anonymous. We do not forgive. We do not forget. Expect us," evokes the omnipresent threat of the locationless hacker. Though their methods, and DDoS in particular, may be fairly simplistic technologically, they are advanced enough to confuse the majority of the public, including law enforcement and the news media, who are happy to assign the "hacker" moniker to any nonmainstream technological practice deemed newsworthy. The Anonymous-as-hacker cultural image is a collaboration of sorts between Anonymous and the media, with Anonymous culture happily playing to type as the news media repeats and reinforces the stereotype. Anonymous' adoption of the hacker-figure, a figure generally interpreted as criminal in the media and popular culture, further reinforces the widely perceived nature of DDoS actions as inherently criminal. This complicates Anonymous' attempts to use DDoS as a form of political activism.

The embrace of the media's antisocial hacker figure is also another performance of dissent on the part of Anonymous. By embodying the ultimate boogeyman of the modern technological age, Anonymous rejects the social order as undesirable and irredeemable. By performing the empowered outcast,[iv] they also perform *symbolic exit*.[22] Anonymous as a culture symbolically exits the mainstream, commercialized internet, overrun with private interests and attempts at state-based governance, and sets itself up as the theatrical

---

[iv]Though the hacker folk devil is unmistakably a thoroughly othered outcast, he is also seen as being a techno-wizard, capable and willing of upsetting the entirety of modern society with a few key strokes.

embodiment of the internet as it could to be: anarchic, absurdist, free of outside interference.ᵛ

Notes

1   Doug McAdam, "The Biographical Consequences of Activism," *American Sociological Review* 54 (1989): 745.

2   McAdam, "Biographical Consequences of Activism," 745.

3   Ibid., 746.

4   Quinn Norton, "Anonymous 101: An introduction to the lulz," Wired, November 2011. Last accessed February 25, 2014, http://www.wired.com/threatlevel/2011/11/anonymous-101; David Auerbach, "Anonymity as Culture: Treatise," *Triple Canopy* 15 (2012). Retrieved from http://canopycanopycanopy. com/15/anonymity_as_culture__treatise. Last accessed February 25, 2014.

5   Norton, "Anonymous 101."

6   Auerbach, "Anonymity as Culture."

7   Coleman, "Our weirdness is free."

8   Gabriella Coleman, "Geek politics and Anonymous," 2011. Retrieved from http://re-publica.de/11/blog/panel/geek-politics-and-anonymous/. Last accessed February 25, 2014.

9   Coleman, "Our weirdness is free."

ᵛGabriella Coleman pointed out in response to an early draft of this section that Anonymous' use of the hacker image is not universal, and has in several instances been rejected by various participants in the culture. This brings to the fore the question of how much of Anonymous' use of the "hacker" identity is a reaction to the media's use of the characterization, and how much is internally developed. It is my view that Anonymous trollishly exploits the media's overuse of the "hacker" image primarily to manipulate the culture's perceived "mystique" by outsiders, and secondarily to maintain an internal, tongue-in-cheek reflection of their own A-culture. But, as with most aspects of Anonymous, these uses of the "hacker" image are not universally accepted.

10 Ibid.; R. Vichot, *"Doing it for the lulz?": Online communities of practice and offline tactical media* (Master's thesis, Georgia Institute of Technology, 2009), 21–5.

11 Gabriella Coleman, "Anonymous: From lulz to collective action," *Media Commons*, April 6, 2011. Last accessed February 25, 2014. Retrieved from http://mediacommons. futureofthebook.org/tne/pieces/anonymous-lulz-collective-action.

12 Coleman, "From lulu to collective action."

13 Know Your Meme, "Dusty the Cat." Last accessed February 2014, http://knowyourmeme.com/memes/events/kenny-glenn-case-dusty-the-cat.

14 Molly Sauter, "Guy Fawkes Mask-ology," *HiLow Brow*, April 30, 2012. Last accessed February 25, 2014, http://hilobrow.com/2012/04/30/mask/.

15 Marco Deseriis, "Is Anonymous a New Form of Luddism? A Comparative Analysis of Industrial Machine Breaking, Computer Hacking, and Related Rhetorical Struggles," *Radical History Review* 117 (2013): 35.

16 Deseriis, "Is Anonymous a New Form of Luddism?," 43.

17 Ricardo Dominguez quoted in Wark, "Toywars."

18 Alessandro Ludovico, "'Error loading . . .' Ten years ago, the first netstrikes took place." Last accessed February 25, 2014, http://www.springerin.at/dyn/heft_text. php?textid=1590&lang=en%5D; Thomas, "Ethics of Hacktivism."

19 Coleman, "From lulz to collective action."

20 James Aho, *This Thing of Darkness: A Sociology of the Enemy* (Seattle, WA: University of Washington Press, 1994).

21 Sauter, "If Hackers Didn't Exist."

22 Tommie Shelby, "Impure Dissent: Hip Hop and the Political Ethics of Marginalized Black Urban Youth," *Youth, New Media, and Political Participation*. Forthcoming (Cambridge, MA: MIT Press).

CHAPTER FIVE

Identity, anonymity, and responsibility: DDoS and the personal

Crowd-based actions, such as DDoSes, blockades, and public marches, are not based on the discreet identities of individual participants to be successful. Rather, the visual spectacle of the mass (or, in the case of DDoS, the imagined spectacle) is more valuable than the individual as a self-contained entity in the greater campaign. Organizers rely on the visual image of streets crowded with marchers to convey the commitment of their supporters, or directly reference huge numbers of potential and actual activists in how they refer to their movements and actions, through evocative titles such as the Million Mom March. Tocqueville called this coming together of individuals the moment when "they are no longer isolated men but a power seen from afar. . . ."[1] As a communicative act, it is the coming together that is of importance. Internally, however, there is still a granularity of identity to be contended with, including the question of anonymity, performed identity, responsibility, and technological elitism.

DDoS actions are hardly the only instance wherein the malleability and concealment of activist identities have become an issue. Recent attempts[2] (some successful, some not) to pass antimask legislation in various jurisdictions serve to demonstrate the popularization of identity concealment as well as the state's deep distrust of the tactic. The assumed ease with which online activists can conceal their identity often attracts criticism,[3] though this critique often runs counter to the historical deployment of identity within activist actions, including DDoS actions.

Critiques of anonymous activism also reveal a tension at the base of the Western conception of political responsibility. Though anonymity can be granted to mainstream political activities, such as the use of the anonymous ballot, those political minorities whose democratic participation has been hamstrung by a failure of the public discourse to seriously consider a specific set of issues, or by outright disenfranchisement are denied the protection of anonymous participation. Instead they are forced into legally and sometimes physically precarious situations as a type of public gauntlet, abusively testing the depth of their commitment to their claims. Similarly, there is little credence given to the idea that moral and political responsibility can attach to protest when performed under identities that are not state-sanctioned. This combination leaves the Western state in the sole position to determine the validity of its critics, not based on the content of their criticism but on the performance of their critical identity. What's more, the simultaneous refusal to accept the validity of anonymous protest coupled with punitive overreaching on the part of the judicial system in response to innovative forms of disruptive civil disobedience has a distinctly chilling effect on the ability of many individuals to participate in the public political discourse. Rather, it encourages the expression of dissent only by those individuals willing to risk everything for the sake of a political point, or in Hannah Arendt's words, it fosters "single-minded fanaticism . . . mak[ing] impossible a rational discussion of the issues at stake."[4]

In short, the emphasis on identity-tied "responsibility," as determined and retributed by the state, which has an interest in discouraging novel forms of dissent, actively suppresses opportunities for wide political participation, discourse, and enfranchisement, rather than encouraging them. Civil disobedience, rather than being welcomed as an alternative mode of political participation, is pushed to the fringes of public political life where its practice becomes more extreme and fanatical, and easier for the political mainstream to dismiss.

This chapter is an attempt to bring to the fore the tensions of identity, responsibility, performance, and exclusion that sit at the core of the political use of DDoS actions. These tensions exist within the use of the tactic itself and in the tactic's interplay with the political processes of a discursive democracy in general.

DDoS and impure dissent

DDoS actions and the theatrics that surround them, particularly those indulged in by groups like Anonymous, can and have often been dismissed as apolitical or antipolitical. The disruptive, trollish nature of the actions, and their seeming incapability at the most fundamental, functional level, to contribute meaningfully to the public democratic discourse, makes the dissent practiced though DDoS actions easy to dismiss. In this way, activist DDoS actions can fall under the umbrella of what Tommie Shelby calls "impure dissent."[5] Impure dissent is that which does not take the form of traditional, morally exemplary civil disobedience or other anticipated forms of protest. Shelby's main subject of analysis is hip-hop, but his analysis leaves room for confrontational, disruptive forms of street activism as well. To Shelby, impure dissent contains a mash-up of legitimate, meaningful political content, and other speech and conduct elements that dramatically break from the norms of typical political speech. It is these other elements that have the potential to undermine or counteract the political content of impure dissent. Shelby notes that these nonpolitical elements can include profanity, epithets, negative stereotypes, or violent or pornographic images.[6]

By both design and practice, activist DDoS actions directly confront the privatized, communicative nature of the modern online space. To again refer to Jodi Dean's theory of communicative capitalism, while it is the nature of the online space to facilitate the additive flow of information, it is the nature of the DDoS action to disrupt that flow and to draw explicit attention to that disruption. DDoS actions can be seen as destructive, antisocial, and informatically deviant enough to completely undermine the intended political message of the action. The continued existence and practice of DDoS actions can be interpreted as dangerously undermining the stability of the online space to such an extent that any use is seen as deeply irresponsible at best, and acutely criminal and threatening at worst. We saw an example of this effect earlier in the news coverage that categorized the EDT as terrorists or criminals.

In a more extreme manifestation of this, Anonymous, and other such groups, purposefully cultivate popular associations with antisocial hacker and trollish personas. The use of the stereotyped hacker persona by Anonymous has a number of uses within the culture, including creating greater community cohesion through performance, aligning the group with a romantic and compelling history, and providing a ready-made hook for the media to latch on to in their reporting of Anonymous actions. However, by taking on such an outlaw persona, Anonymous also recuses itself from the pantheon of traditional civic actors. The hacker outlaw is a politically impure actor, a potential threat who lives on the fringes of respectable society. By taking on that character's mantle, Anonymous renders their dissent both politically and morally "impure." The inflection or tone of their outward messaging is also seen as deeply problematic, as it often incorporates cursing, vulgar humor, epithets, and a host of content unsuitable to polite conversation. Anonymous' status as impure dissenters makes it difficult for them to communicate their political message to those outside the culture, but should not in and of itself invalidate their dissent.

The interruptive nature of DDoS actions means that the role it can serve within a discursive democracy is limited. Those who use the tactic are functionally incapable *in that moment* from participating in the democratic process as a discussant. It is here that DDoS actions are often criticized as a "heckler's veto,"[7] a contribution that is counter to the practices of a discursive democracy. But a disruptive act of civil disobedience serves to alert the wider public that the normal channels of participation have failed for a certain population. The lack of signal that is the external manifestation of an activist DDoS action should be interpreted as making space for unheard dissent. That making-of-space, the creation of an awkward silence in the constant whirl of communicative capitalism, is not a breakdown of "authentic deliberation" but a chance to "reinstate a deliberative environment" which has suffered a participatory breakdown.[8]

As previously mentioned, a primary motivation for the EDT and *the electrohippies* during the DDoS actions of the late 1990s was to establish the internet as a viable space for civil disobedience and dissent. *The electrohippies* stated in one of their initial papers defending the use of DDoS actions:

> Whilst the Internet was originally a place of discussion and networking, the invasion of corporate interests into this space has changed the perceptions of what the purpose of the Internet is. Some believe that the Internet is no longer a "public" space—it has become a domain for the large corporations to peddle their particular brand of unsustainable consumerism. For many this is unacceptable. . . . Whatever the views of particular people about the development of e-commerce on the 'Net, we must not ignore the fact that as another part of society's public space the Internet will be used by groups and individuals as a means of protests. There is no practical difference between cyberspace and the street in terms of how people use the 'Net.[9]

However, despite their aspirations, the commercialization and privatization of the internet continued. As of 2013, the online space is, as it stands, thoroughly privatized. Public spaces, as they are understood to exist in the physical world under the guise of parks, sidewalks and roadways, do not exist online. As such, the expectations of speech rights online follow, not the norms of public spaces, but the norms of private property. The "public forum doctrine," which was discussed earlier,[i] governs both the law and the social norms here.

Of the three, sometimes four, broad categories identified by the US Supreme Court, the most permissive in terms of speech restrictions is the "traditional public forum": streets, parks, sidewalks, town commons, and other areas traditionally recognized as being held in common for the public good. The most restrictive is private property, in so much as the owners of private property are relatively free in the restrictions they can place on the speech of others when it takes place on their property.[10]

The internet is not a "traditional public forum." Online outlets for speech, such as blogging platforms, social networks, forums, or other wellsprings of user-generated content are privately owned. US-based ISPs could be subject to liability if they do not properly police their users' content. The internet has developed into a zone of modern life lacking some crucial First Amendment protections. While the freedom of the press is relatively well protected in the online space, the rights of assembly and speech of the average individual remains unprotected. Given the internet's current role as a basic outlet of personal expression, association, and communication, this is deeply troubling. While protest taking place in the various public fora in the physical world have a foundation of history and legal doctrine to support their legitimacy as valid and protected political speech, actions that take place in the online

---

[i] See Chapter 2.

sphere can only ever infringe on privately held property. The architecture of the network does not, as of yet, support spaces held in common.

As a privately held public sphere, disruptive acts of civil disobedience online will always be in conflict with dearly held doctrines of private property. This conflict has a physical-world parallel. The initial Occupy Wall Street camp was established at Zucotti Park, a "privately-held public space" that is ostensibly available for public use but still subject to the potential restrictions of private property. The free speech obligations/protections provided by such spaces are legally murky. Without substantial legal precedent supporting the rights activists to stage potentially disruptive political actions, the use of DDoS as a tactic in and of itself has the potential to render the activist action impure by coming into conflict with private property rights without the established cultural and legal protections that have developed around physical-world civil disobedience. This is disastrous for the development of civil disobedience online. By being continually compared with activism in a sphere with substantially different norms of property and speech (i.e., the physical world), civil disobedience online consistently comes out tainted by perceived criminality or bullying behavior. In this case, it is primarily the evolved constraints of the network itself that render DDoS activist actions impure.

Identity, anonymity, and responsibility within protest

Early groups explicitly revealed and advertised the identity of the organizers of DDoS actions. This followed the position of the EDT and *the electrohippies* that DDoS actions were a direct adaptation of sit-ins and other street-based tactics, which incorporate a give-and-take with the state and law enforcement into their operational logic. However, this view of identification, responsibility, and state participation hasn't held in more recent DDoS actions. In particular, Anonymous, which maintains anonymity as an aspect of their culture, refuses to buy the claim that the state is engaging with digital activism in good faith. Moreover, Anonymous for the most part refuses to acknowledge that national governments, particularly that of the United States, have any legitimate role in governing the internet at all.

Both the EDT and *the electrohippies* explicitly revealed and advertised their identities as organizers of DDoS actions. This tactic of preemptive identification was yet another aspect of their adaptation of physical-world protest tactics for the online space. As articulated by *the electrohippies*:

> We have nothing to hide, as we believe that our purpose is valid, and so we do not seek to hide it from any authorities who seek to surveil us. Likewise, we do not try to bury our identities from law enforcement authorities, any authority could, if it chose to, track us down in a few hours. . . . The right to take action against another entity on the 'Net must be balanced with the principle of accountability.[11]

The electrohippies claimed that by openly revealing their identities as organizers, they could be held accountable by the public whose participation they were seeking. Further, they claimed that such accountability ensured that the tactic would only be used in "justifiable" situations: "If the group using the tool do not feel they can be open about its use then we consider that their action cannot be considered justifiable. A justifiable action cannot be mounted from behind the mask of anonymity."[12] They also viewed the practice as a hedge against accusations of terrorism or criminality by the state or in the press.

In their essay analyzing their use of "client-side distributed denial of service" and in other writings, *the electrohippies* repeatedly frame their use of DDoS as a natural continuation of existing constitutional rights. Like the EDT, they saw the online space as a complementary, equally valid theater of activism to the physical world, and approached it as such with the assumption that if previously accepted activist practices, like sit-ins, were symmetrically adapted to the online space, the reactions of the state could be predicted.

These groups did not require participants to publicly identify themselves to the same degree as organizers; *the electrohippies* recommended the use of anonymous, throw-away e-mail addresses for their WTO e-mail bombing campaign. However, the groups did acknowledge the likelihood and potential consequences of being identified as participants in these actions, as stated on the EDT's website, still using street activism as the dominant frame of reference:

WARNING: This is a Protest, it is not a game, it may have personal consequences as in any off-line political manifestation on the street: Based on critiques from the Heart Hackers and other individuals about FloodNet:

1. Your IP address will be harvested by the government during any FloodNet action. When you click and enter FloodNet your name and political position will be made known to the authorities.

(Similar to having your picture taking during a protest action on the street.)

2. Possible damage to your machine may occur because of your participation in the FloodNet action.

(Just as in a street action—the police may come and hurt you.)

3. FloodNet clogs bandwidth and may make it difficult for many individuals using small pipelines around the world to get information. FloodNet may not impact the targeted website specifically as much as it disrupts traffic going to the targeted website, i.e. problems for Internet routes to the site.

(This also happens when people take to the streets. Individuals may find themselves unable to get to work or buy a newspaper because of the action. FloodNet actions are short term and only disturb bandwidth during the time of the manifestation. The Electronic Disturbance Theater feels that even if FloodNet only functions as a symbolic action, that is enough to make the collective presence of activists felt beyond the electronic networks.)

We hope that when you join our Virtual Sit-in's in support of global communities of resistance, you will take the above information to heart.[13]

The EDT and *the electrohippies*' reliance on physical-world structures of accountability indicate a belief that the assumptions of physical-world activism would hold true for activism in the online space as well, particularly assumptions around interactions with the state and its agents. The EDT's warning acknowledges the expected role law enforcement typically plays in street activism. In this conception, the state serves as a theatrical antagonist and legitimator of dissent by virtue of their reaction: as stated by Jerry Rubin in 1969, "The cops are a necessary part of any demonstration theater. When you are planning a demonstration, always include a role for the cops. Cops legitimize demonstrations."[14] Similarly, in his original conception of civil disobedience, when Thoreau says, "Under a government which imprisons any unjustly, the true place for a just man is also a prison,"[15] he values the spectacle of the state imprisoning a just man for its value as an illustration of the injustice of the state, to which others may react. William Smith calls this a "moral dialogue with authorities" in which the protestors, law enforcement, and general citizenry are all participants.[16] In so much as activists can provoke a punitive reaction from the state, they can in turn also trigger a public dialogue as to the appropriateness of that response.[17]

Symbolic activism of the type practiced by the EDT and other co-temporaneous groups requires an interaction with the state to be effective. Though the reaction of the state to novel forms of dissent is not entirely predictable, it's clear from their writings that the EDT expected the state's response to fit broadly within the mold of its typical responses to street activism. They expected to be treated as activists. Like street activists, the EDT's actions were occasionally met with a militarized response: one of the EDT's FloodNet-powered actions prompted an aggressive "counter-hack"[18] from the Pentagon, an action that was criticized as being an unreasonable cyber-attack against US-based civilians.[19] This notwithstanding, the EDT maintained, through its literature and practice an assumption that their actions would be treated as political in nature. By refusing to conceal their own legal identities, and by not providing their participants with the technical knowledge and means to evade identification, the EDT maintained a space for the state to participate as a useful actor in the processes they were trying to impact.

Contrary to this, Anonymous holds anonymity to be a core aspect of its culture. Anonymity is the default assumption, both in interpersonal interactions and particularly when engaging in public-facing actions. Individuals who out themselves are derisively referred to as "name-fags" and can sometimes receive a quite aggressive reaction.[20] Auerbach, as previously noted, lays the credit for this cultural development at the feet of the technological systems upon which the Anonymous culture was built, fast-moving message boards that were ephemeral and unsigned by nature. While this explains where the value originated, it does not explain why it has penetrated so deeply into the culture's activist activities, nor why it has persisted at the levels of both technological systems and cultural practice.

Anonymous' maintenance of anonymity in the face of established activist practice in part indicates a refusal to accept the assumptions of earlier groups. While the EDT and *the electrohippies* inherently granted the rights of states to govern the online space as they govern the physical world, Anonymous does not. Anonymous' political conception of the internet, in so much as it coherently stands, is more akin to that articulated by John Perry Barlow in his 1996 "A Declaration of the Independence of Cyberspace":

Governments of the Industrial World, you weary giants of flesh and steel, I come from Cyberspace, the new home of Mind. On behalf of the future, I ask you of the past to leave us alone. You are not welcome among us. You have no sovereignty where we gather.

We have no elected government, nor are we likely to have one, so I address you with no greater authority than that with which liberty itself always speaks. I declare the global social space we are building to be naturally independent of the tyrannies you seek to impose on us. You have no moral right to rule us nor do you possess any methods of enforcement we have true reason to fear.

Governments derive their just powers from the consent of the governed. You have neither solicited nor received ours. We did not invite you. You do not know us, nor do you know our world. Cyberspace does not lie within your borders. Do not think that you can build it, as though it were a public construction project. You cannot. It is an act of nature and it grows itself through our collective actions.[21]

Anonymity, in this context, becomes a political response to the perceived illegitimacy of state governance online. During the Operation Chanology street protests against the Church of Scientology, Anonymous encouraged participants to wear masks to protect themselves against later harassment by the Church. During Operation Payback and later actions, the use of anonymity during a DDoS action incorporates within it a refusal to engage with traditional scripts of activism that inherently legitimize the role of the state and of law enforcement within the action.

In addition to simply denying the legitimacy of the state in governing dissent online, anonymity as an online activist practice contains within it a belief that the state and corporate actors targeted by the activists will not respond in good faith.[22] Earlier groups drew on the history and scripts of street activism to anticipate interactions with states and law enforcement. Anonymous, operating some 10 years later, draws on a much different history of state antagonism toward hackers, DRM battles, and post-9/11 War on Terror surveillance and policing of dissent. Given the tradition in the United States of frankly ridiculous, overreaching CFAA-enabled computer crime prosecutions, this assumption of bad faith is not unreasonable. This is similar to the rationale behind the use of masks by Black Bloc actors during street actions. Thompson quotes Black Bloc activists citing "protect[ing] ourselves from illegal police surveillance" and "provid[ing] cover for activists engaged in illegal actions during the demo"[23] as reasons for the use of masks during street protests. The logic is clear: if your aim is to commit a political act not recognized as a privileged political act by the state, then taking actions to prevent yourself, as a political actor, from being assigned the role of criminal actor by the state is reasonable.

Anonymity as an outward-facing cultural practice strengthens the "relational equality" between the individual participant and the greater cultural movement.[24] As mentioned before, Anonymous relies on the perception of an inexhaustible mass for much of its rhetorical bite. The identical-ness of its masked, technologically anonymized participants foster a sense of omnipresence, the type of "improperly-named" mob noted by Deseriis.[25] Outward-facing anonymity prevents outside actors, like the media, from focusing on and privileging charismatic actors. Anonymous values the optics of the mass, the "hive," while simultaneously continuing to value internally individuality and individual initiative.[26]

That said, though anonymity is the goal during these actions, it is not always achieved. The most popular versions of the LOIC DDoS tool used by Anonymous in Operation PayBack made no effort to cover its users' digital tracks. More sophisticated DDoS tools will "spoof" IP addresses, generating a fake IP address to assign to the packets the program sends out, or take other steps to prevent the target of an action from tracing the packets back home. However, all packets sent with LOIC are tagged with the IP address of the sender. ISPs maintain records of the IP addresses of computers on their network and can match those IP records to the real names and addresses of their subscribers. Law enforcement can and often does subpoena those records when pursuing computer crime prosecutions. It was possible for an individual using LOIC, without taking additional security measures, to be identified on the basis of information contained in the packets he or she sent. The EDT's FloodNet tool and the adapted version used by *the electrohippies*, also did not utilize any measures to mask the identity of participants. However, this should be seen as an extension of those groups' integration of physical-world/legal identity into their actions. Given Anonymous' history of anonymous action and the emphasis placed on anonymity within Anonymous culture, that LOIC does not conceal users' identities is more likely to be a mistake or hallmark of an inexperienced developer rather than an intentional decision.

For a sophisticated user, this security flaw is relatively easy to detect by glancing at the tool's source code or by testing the tool against a known machine (such as one's own server). However, most of those participating in the December 2010 DDoS campaign were not sophisticated users. They were recent additions to the Anonymous DDoS army, "n00bs" or "newfags" in Anonymous parlance. Whereas an experienced user may have been aware that running LOIC through a proxy or a spoofed IP address would provide some measure of protection from the security flaws in the tool, it is unlikely that someone new to digital activism would be aware those tools existed or would understand how to operate them. Very few of the tutorials available online made mention of any of these options. In fact, many of the FAQs and tutorials reassured users that they were unlikely to be caught using the tool as is, or if they were caught, they were unlikely to face any serious trouble. These statements were often factually inaccurate and based on a faulty understanding of how servers operated. One FAQ reads, in part:

Q: Will I get caught/arrested for using it?
A: *Chances are next to zero* [italics added]. Just blame [sic] you have a virus, or simply deny any knowledge of it.[27]

The media also picked up this line, and repeated it extensively, as in this article by Joel Johnson of Gizmodo:

> What is LOIC? It's a pushbutton application that can be controlled by a central user to launch a flood of killer internet packets with *little risk to the user* [italics added]. Because a DDoS knocks everything offline—at least when it works as intended—*the log files that would normally record each incoming connection typically just don't work* [italics added]. And even if they do, many LOIC users claim that another user was on their network or that their machine was part of a bot net—a DDoS client delivered by virus that performs like a hivemind LOIC, minus the computer owner actually knowing they are participating.[28]

In this article, Johnson mistakenly states that a server targeted by a DDoS action would not log the IP addresses on the incoming packets, a statement that is simply inaccurate. In fact, PayPal and other Operation Payback targets kept extensive logs of traffic to their websites, logs that law enforcement used to target participants for searches and arrests.

As a result, it is probable that many newly recruited Anons used LOIC to join in on large-scale DDoS actions against financial institutions, such as PayPal, Visa, and MasterCard, without taking any security precautions whatsoever. In the coming months, dozens of those individuals would be arrested and charged under the Computer Fraud and Abuse Act.[29] It was later revealed that those arrests were based on a master list of IP addresses collected by PayPal as its servers were struck by a massive wave of DDoS actions on December 9 and 10, 2010,[30] something sites such as Gizmodo had previously claimed was impossible. Despite criticism that activist DDoS actions are cheaper or easier or "less risky" than other forms of activism, these actions can be extremely legally risky, due to an insistence on the part of the judicial system that activist DDoS actions be treated as criminal felonies, not political acts.

An insistence that legal identity be tied to dissenting speech or disruptive activism benefits a state with an interest in tracking and suppressing those activities. The US Supreme Court has noted the value of anonymous political speech, going so far as to recognize a right to anonymous pamphleteering, in the tradition of the anonymous and pseudonymous writings of Thomas Paine and the founding fathers.[31] Just as an interruptive DDoS can open an opportunity for dissenting speech, the ability to engage in anonymous activism can create for individuals the opportunity to dissent. A chance to protest that is tracked and monitored is, for most of the public, no chance at all. It restricts the opportunities for dissent and disruption to the few who can bear the state-determined cost. As Tressie McMillan Cottom notes, "The penalty for raising hell is not the same for everyone."[32] An insistence on exposing oneself to legal threat as a cost to dissenting speech prices most people out of the discursive democracy market, regardless of their views. A democratic society that recognizes the right of citizens to political participation, and recognizes the value of civil disobedience as a reasonable and necessary manifestation of that right, must in turn recognize that anonymous civil disobedience and dissent is vital to the expression of those rights. Otherwise, we are using the excuse of "responsibility" to deny individuals their right to full political participation.

Accessibility in technologically defined tactical spaces

DDoS actions were taken up by digitally enabled activists as a more accessible, less geographically bounded tactic for activist expression than physical-world actions. While the CAE saw the move to the online space as tracking the movements of structures of power to their new abode,[33] later groups saw it as a way to lower the barriers to entry. As mass DDoS actions have continued to develop tactically over the years, different groups have continued to adapt it so that it is easier for individuals to participate. This adaptation occurs both on the level of tool design and information distribution, but also at a community level. During Operation Payback, for example, LOIC tutorials began popping up on YouTube and other locations around the web. Though it would be impossible to get an exact figure, a YouTube search conducted in April 2013 for "LOIC tutorial" yields thousands of results. One video, "How to Use LOIC (Low Orbit Ion Cannon)", uploaded in mid-November 2010, had been viewed over 80,000 times by December 12, 2010, and had been viewed over 250,000 by April 2013.[34]

However, any efforts to further spread the tactic will be hampered by its very nature as a high bandwidth digital tactic. Its use is restricted to relatively affluent populations with unrestricted access to digital technology and high quality, reliable internet connectivity. Most DDoS tools in use from 2010 on must be downloaded and run from a computer, though other, less popular versions exist that can be run from a website or a smart phone. This automatically excludes potential participants in areas with poor internet connectivity, or those who don't own their own computers and must rely on machines at schools, libraries, or cybercafes where they aren't able to download and install new programs.

In some ways, the earlier webpage based tools like the EDT's FloodNet may have been more diversely accessible than tools like LOIC or its successors. The early actions were also scheduled to last for only short amounts of time, at most an hour or two, to accommodate the restrictions and expense of participating in an action over a dial-up connection. The "occupation"-style DDoS actions organized by Anonymous, conversely, have run for days through broadband, cable, DSL or fiber connections. So though advances in connectivity and computing power have made it possible for actions to last longer (and potentially have a greater impact on their target), taking advantage of those advancements can severely limit the potential participant pool.

This has resulted in natural narrowing of trigger events for activist DDoS actions to mostly internet- or technology-oriented events. While the EDT, *the electrohippies* and others targeted the online representations of state governments and multinational organizations, responding to cross-border issues of policy and globalization, Anonymous and its kin most frequently respond to events that occur in the online space itself. Operation Chanology was triggered by the Church of Scientology's attempts to remove a video of Tom Cruise from various websites. Operation Payback, both in its initial and Avenge Assange segments, was provoked by actions taken online which affected "internet native" entities, like the Pirate Bay or Wikileaks. This focus results in a further narrowing of the potentially interested participant pool. So while DDoS actions were and are often now deployed with intentions of dramatically expanding the activist population, accessibility and cultural issues often create severe barriers to that goal.

Notes

1   Alexis de Tocqueville, *Democracy in America*, trans. Harvey C. Mansfield and Delba Winthrop (Chicago: University of Chicago Press, 2002).

2   Canada's Bill C-309 is the most recent example of this type of restrictive legislation, which carries a potential penalty of 10 years in prison. Austria, Denmark, France, Germany, Spain, Sweden, Switzerland, Ukraine, the UK, and several jurisdictions within the US have all had anti-mask legislation on the books, or have passed and subsequently repealed such laws in the last decade.

3   The most common version of this criticism is that anonymous political speech cannot carry the same weight as non-anonymous speech because it entails less risk or because it encourages bad behavior and abusive speech. This view can be seen in comments made by Randi Zuckerberg of Facebook,

Google CEO Eric Schmidt, and others. The opposition of tech executives to anonymous speech on, ostensibly, grounds of moral and political responsibility is striking due to their control of the very structures of expression that many people rely on.

4 Arendt, *Crises of the Republic*, 67.

5 Shelby, "Impure Dissent," 7.

6 Ibid., 8–9.

7 Siva Vaidhyanathan (@sivavaid), "@ethanz @oddletters DDoS is the heckler's veto." April 5, 2013. Last accessed February 2014, https://twitter.com/sivavaid/status/320224482289655808.

8 Smith, *Civil Disobedience and Deliberative Democracy*, 60–83.

9 DJNZ/electrohippies, "Client-side Distributed Denial-of-Service: Valid campaign tactic or terrorist act?" *Electrohippies Occasional Paper*, February 2000. Last accessed February 25, 2014, www.fraw.org.uk/projects/electrohippies/archive/op-01/html.

10 McPhail, et al., "Policing Protest in the United States."

11 DJNZ/electrohippies, "Client-side Distributed Denial-of-Service."

12 Ibid.

13 Carmin Karasic and Brett Stalbaum, "FloodNet Warning," September 1998. Last accessed February 25, 2014. Archived at http://www.thing.net/~rdom/zapsTactical/warning.htm.

14 Jerry Rubin, "Yippie Manifesto," *Free Pamphlet Series #1* (Vineyard Haven, MA: Evergreen Review, Inc. 1969).

15 Thoreau, "Civil Disobedience."

16 Smith, *Civil Disobedience and Deliberative Democracy*, 76.

17 Ibid.

18 This military-grade response is analyzed in detail in Chapter 7.

19 Meikle, *FutureActive*, 153.

20 Coleman, "Our weirdness is free."

21 John Perry Barlow, "A Declaration of Independence for Cyberspace," February 8, 1996. Last accessed February 25, 2014. Archived at https://projects.eff.org/~barlow/Declaration-Final.html.

22 Shelby, "Impure dissent."

23   Thompson, *Black Bloc*, 57.

24   Ollman quoted in Thompson, *Black Bloc*, 56.

25   Deseriis, "Is Anonymous a New Form of Luddism?"

26   Coleman, "Our weirdness is free."

27   "Operation Payback setup guide," December 2010. Last accessed February 27, 2014, http://pastehtml.com/view/1c8i33u.html.

28   Joel Johnson, "What is LOIC?" *Gizmodo.com*, December 8, 2010. Last accessed February 25, 2014, http://gizmodo.com/5709630/what-is-loic.

29   Kim Zetter, "Feds arrest 14 'Anonymous' suspects over PayPal attack, raid dozens more," *Wired*, June 2011. Last accessed February 25, 2014, http://www.wired.com/threatlevel/2011/07/paypal-hack-arrests/.

30   Kevin Poulsen, "In Anonymous raids, feds work from list of top 1,000 protesters," *Wired*, June 2011. Last accessed February 25, 2014, http://www.wired.com/threatlevel/2011/07/op_payback/.

31   McIntyre v. Ohio Elections Comm'n (93–986), 514 U.S. 334 (1995).

32   Tressie McMillan Cottom, "Academic Cowards and Why I Don't Write Anonymously," http://tressiemc.com/2014/01/21/academic-cowards-and-why-i-dont-write-anonymously/.

33   Critical Art Ensemble, *Electronic Civil Disobedience*.

34   This video and its metrics can be viewed at https://www.youtube.com/watch?v=sQRu-J3f_Kw and was last accessed on April 23, 2013.

CHAPTER SIX

LOIC will tear us apart: DDoS tool development and design

In activist DDoS actions, the tool used sets the first level of community, literally serving as the collective launch point for the action. Participants will often all use one tool or one of a family of tools recommended by the organizers. Though there have been several different tools used during these actions, some ad hoc, some more polished, the two most notable tools for activist DDoS actions have been the EDT's FloodNet tool, and Anonymous' LOIC. Because both these tools were released open source, other groups in the case of FloodNet and participants within the Anonymous collective in the case of LOIC were able to progressively adapt these tools for the needs of any given action. This adaptability extended the life and influence of these tools past the initial actions they were developed for. Through being adopted and adapted by other groups, individuals, and actions, the successive versions of these tools act as a connective string of influence, as the technological affordances, design assumptions, specific functionalities, and interface choices impact each new action that uses them.

In this chapter, I trace the development of the EDT's FloodNet and the Anonymous' family of LOIC DDoS tools.

I'm particularly interested in complex of language, memes, and references used in the interface design of these tools and their paratextual materials, such as tutorial videos and how-tos, as well as scheduling and recruitment documentation. The specific language and references used can show not only the targeted user group for the tool (and thus the intended participants for the action), but can also give clues as to the lineage of the tool and the specific development of the groups using it.

The previous chapter was an attempt to address DDoS actions at the level of social movement theory. This chapter takes the technological tools used during these actions as a base for the analysis of these actions. Rather than looking at them on a purely technological level, this chapter examines these tools in the context of activist actions and communities, at how their existence impacts campaigns. The design and affordances of the tool used can define a variety of aspects of the actions, including the level of engagement expected from participants, as well as indicating, after the fact, the types of individuals who were recruited and active, and the amount of political "seriousness" indicated by the action.

The Electronic Disturbance Theater and FloodNet

FloodNet was developed in 1998 by EDT members Carmin Karasic and Brett Stalbaum, with Stalbaum as the primary developer and Karasic handling the interface design and testing. Written in Java, the tool exploited something called the "applet reload function," with the tool requesting a reload of webpages or sections of webpages from the targeted server several times a minute. In the earliest version of the tool, these reload requests were triggered every 7 seconds. Later versions were able to increase the request load to once every 3 seconds.

FloodNet was a browser-based tool. Participants navigated to a specific webpage that hosted the tool, selected certain parameters, often from a drop-down menu, and allowed the tool to run in the background. "Messages" of a kind could also be sent to the targeted server. FloodNet could send requests for specific files to the targeted server. A request for "human rights" would generate a "404_file not found" message in the server's logs: "human_rights not found on this server."[1] Such a message could be found by a systems administrator later. This performative "messaging" functionality would appear in Anonymous' LOIC tool. This type of messaging is not particular useful as a mode of communication. It's very unlikely that anyone other than a systems administrator will ever see these logged messages. So these messages and the messaging functionality of the FloodNet tool itself is best viewed as an outlet for the activists themselves. A small point of individually determined personal expression in a tool that otherwise provided few opportunities to stray from the choreography of the action.

The EDT held 13 pro-Zapatista actions in 1998 using FloodNet, targeting websites ranging from those of the Clinton White House and the Pentagon to those of Mexican president Ernesto Zedillo and the Frankfurt Stock Exchange, with mixed success. These actions attracted up to 18,000 participants but did not generate much focused media attention.[2] On January 1, 1999, the source code for the FloodNet tool was released, allowing other groups to use the tool in their own actions. It was this version that was adapted by *the electrohippies* for their 1999 WTO action, and by the "Deportation Class Action" activists in 2001. Its design was simple and for the most part undifferentiated version to version. Participants either selected a target from a preselected list of targets, or the tool could be set up such that target selection was automatic. Participants were not asked to manually input targeting information. The only free user-input aspect of the tool, as mentioned above, was the text field where one could type their message to the server.

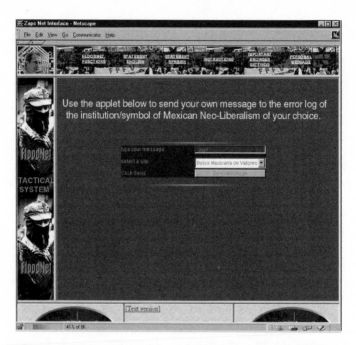

FIGURE 1 *A screen shot of the web-based version of the EDT's FloodNet DDoS tool.*

Figure 1 is the version of FloodNet used by the EDT during their pro-Zapatista actions in 1998. These actions were strictly scheduled, running for only 1 or 2 hours on a given day. The language used in the interface clearly marks the tool as belonging to a particular population of activists and artists who were familiar with the language and practices of street and media activism. The tool invites users to "send your own message to the error log of the institution/symbol of Mexican Neo-Liberalism of your choice," specialized language that creates a gulf between those who already understand it and those who do not. The tool does not appear to have been designed to appeal to users who were not already interested in and informed about the issue at hand. This impression is underscored by the methods by which the EDT publicized its actions: through mailing lists and message boards frequented by media activists and special interest lists devoted to South America, the Zapatista struggle, and other related topics. In its attempt to translate the physical-world sit-in to the online space, FloodNet clings to a one-person/one-computer operations model, refusing to augment the resulting flow of traffic with tools such as botnets (volunteer or otherwise) or other traffic amplification exploits.[3] This tied the ethical validity of their actions, and eventually of DDoS itself as a tactic, to how closely they could be compared to physical-world actions. It also added another point of contention and confusion between these internet-enabled activists, and hacktivists, who saw FloodNet as technologically inefficient and poorly designed from a network standpoint.[4] However, for the EDT, the technological inefficiency of FloodNet was a feature, not a bug, as it allowed the "voice" of each participant to be meaningfully present in a collective action, without running the risk of being drowned out by automated machine noise. FloodNet hamstrung the efficiency of the machine in order to place a higher value on the input of the human participants. As we will see next, not all those who followed the EDT's path cared to follow this logic.

Anonymous, Operation Payback and LOIC

Operation Payback began in September of 2010 as what Anonymous claimed was a retaliatory DDoS campaign targeting the Motion Picture Association of America (MPAA), the Recording Industry Association of America (RIAA), and other targets after those organizations had (according to Anonymous) hired an Indian firm, Aiplex to DDoS the Pirate Bay, a file-sharing website.[5] The MPAA and the RIAA are the major lobbying groups for the content industry in the United States and have a history of litigiously opposing what they consider to be the theft of their content via peer-to-peer file-sharing sites, such as the Pirate Bay. Individuals within Anonymous argued the DDoS actions by the RIAA and the MPAA as a threat to file sharing and torrenting and as a further example of the abuses perpetrated by the corporate content and IP industries.[i] Specifically, the use of DDoS tactics by the RIAA in an attempt to completely disable the Pirate Bay, which only existed in its online state, while Anons had been imprisoned for launching DDoS actions against the websites of the Church of Scientology, which existed primarily in the physical world as a complex organization, was presented as breathtakingly hypocritical. A group of Anons called AnonOps led the DDoS actions against the RIAA, MPAA, and Aiplex, which continued for more than a month. All three targets reported downtime.[6]

While it's clear that Aiplex had engaged in the past in for-hired DDoS actions against torrent sites including the Pirate Bay, it is far from clear that the MPAA and the RIAA ever specifically hired Aiplex to target the Pirate Bay. This first phase of Operation Payback, properly called Operation Payback is a Bitch, which had initially been conceived as an anti-ACTA protest, switched to targeting Aiplex after the publication and global spread of an article from an Indian newspaper wherein the managing director admitted that the firm was often hired by the film industry to stop the pirating of material through various means. After a first strike against Aiplex, considered by Gabriella Coleman to be a botnet powered wildcat action directed by just one person, Anonymous launched a series of collective actions against Aiplex, the MPAA, and RIAA, the International Federation of the Phonographic Industry, and a British IP law firm. These actions relied on the narrative that these lobbying

---

[i]Torrenting is a method of peer-to-peer file sharing that allows individuals to download large files, broken up into pieces, from several different servers at the same time.

organizations had hired Aiplex to conduct extralegal DDoS attacks against the Pirate Bay. This narrative was widely accepted by both Anons and the press, which repeated the story extensively.[7]

The ease with which this narrative was accepted tells us something about how these initial stages of Operation Payback were viewed. Under this lens, the motivation behind the attack-for-hire on the Pirate Bay was to remove content from the internet, in this case, torrent files available on the Pirate Bay's servers.[8] The MPAA and others are cast, not as wanting to call attention to the issue of online file sharing but, rather, as wanting to obliterate the informatic entity known as the Pirate Bay. This would not be an entirely unrealistic course of action for them to take. A 2007 article in *Wired* reported that in 2005, the MPAA hired a hacker to exfiltrate confidential information from the servers of TorrentSpy, a popular torrent tracker.[9] That the MPAA would fight dirty to combat online movie piracy is far from unlikely.

The Pirate Bay and the MPAA are different types of organizational entities. The Pirate Bay functions like a directory, a compendium of paths to data. It has no public presence beyond its internet presence and serves no function beyond making certain files available to users. Alternatively, the RIAA and the MPAA do not exist primarily online. Their websites are little more than informational homepages. No business is conducted there, and the hearts of the organizations do not reside online. The stated motivation for the Anonymous actions on the MPAA and the RIAA was to disrupt their operations and cause the organizations to spend money and resources fending off the DDoS actions,[10] but the primary benefit of the actions lay in the media attention and new participants it attracted, who sympathized with Anonymous' views and could participate in future actions. It functioned, in part because of media coverage, as a recruitment drive.

December 6, 2010, marked the beginning second stage of Operation Payback, sometimes known as Operation Avenge Assange. This second wave of DDoS actions targeted organizations and individuals Anonymous believed were acting against the interests of WikiLeaks, either by cutting off its channels of financial support, by refusing to provide hosting to the website and its domain name, or by speaking out against the organization publicly. Over the course of 4 days, Anonymous launched DDoS actions against over a dozen sites, causing downtime and service outages at several.[11] These actions were powered by volunteers using the LOIC DDoS tool and were augmented by nonvolunteer botnets.[12]

The program used during the Anonymous DDoS action, LOIC, is similar to FloodNet but differs in significant ways. By the time LOIC was developed, the basic functionality of automated DDoS programs had evolved to match improvements in website infrastructure. Beyond that, more important shifts had been made in the areas of community development and open-source coding projects and platforms. LOIC was forked several times, allowing the creation of different versions of the tool adapted to the needs and preferences of different user groups.[ii] Not only did LOIC represent an evolutionary step in the development of activist-oriented DDoS tools overall, but it continued to evolve within the context of Anonymous during the course of Operation Chanology and Operation Payback.

LOIC was originally developed and distributed by a developer using the handle praetox[13] as a server "stress-testing" tool. It's likely that this tool was never strictly intended to be used as a legitimate stress-testing tool, and the classification is instead a useful cover for the tool's actual purpose: to disrupt the websites of others. A number of different versions of the tool based on praetox's original code were developed, some of which added new functionalities to the tool or adapted it to run in different environments.

[ii]To "fork" an open-source software project is to take the source code from one project and independently develop it, thus creating a separate piece of software. The LOIC forks reflect distinct differences in affordances and design.

I group those projects that are based on praetox's original code and that retain the LOIC name and the core functionality under the name LOIC. I will be examining some of the forks individually, as they reflect the previously discussed shifts in the Anonymous population, strategy, and political goals. The evolution of this particular tool further serves as a case study in the attempt to mainstream DDoS as a tool of political protest.

A forked comparison: abatishchev and NewEraCracker

When the first version of LOIC was made available on the internet is difficult to determine, but it was in use in 2008, during Operation Chanology.[14] In the next 2 years, different versions of the project began popping up on open-source software development sites. Versions of LOIC could be downloaded from SourceForge and GitHub, popular open-source software repositories. Individuals could also add code to LOIC projects on these sites (a practice known as "committing code" or "code commits"), leave comments for the developers, request features, and report bugs. As such, they were far more social in their development and distribution than FloodNet. Use of those development community websites meant that more people concurrently participated in the development of LOIC, making it possible for the tools to more accurately reflect the needs, whims, and tastes of the target audience. By December of 2010, versions of LOIC could be run on Windows, Mac, and Linux PCs as well as Android phones and jailbroken iPhones. A version called JS LOIC, or JavaScript LOIC, ran like the EDT's FloodNet application from within a web browser; the user was not required to download or install anything.[15]

The most widely downloaded versions of LOIC in December of 2010 were posted to SourceForge and GitHub by abatishchev (Figure 4) and NewEraCracker (Figure 5), respectively. These two

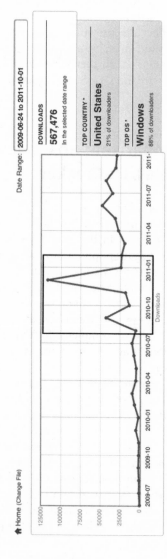

FIGURE 2 *This SourceForge chart shows downloads of the abatishchev LOIC from June 2009 through October 1, 2011. The first spike in the highlighted portion is September 2010, at the start of Operation Payback. The second, larger spike is December 2010. From September through December 2010, abatishchev's LOIC was downloaded 191,781 times. Retrieved from http://sourceforge.net/projects/loic/files/stats/timeline.*

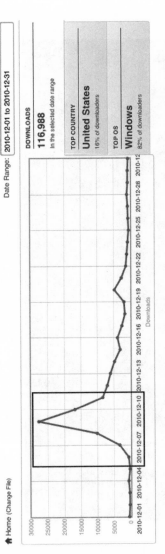

FIGURE 3 *This SourceForge chart shows the December 2010 downloads of abatishchev's LOIC program. The highlighted portion shows the duration of Operation Payback's Avenge Assange actions, starting with an action against the Swedish banking website postfinance.ch on December 6 and ending with an action against conservatives4palin.com on December 10. During the campaign's weeklong run in December 2010, abatishchev's LOIC was downloaded 58,795 times, accounting for half the total downloads for the month, and just under a third of the total downloads from the September through December 2010 period. Retrieved from http:// sourceforge.net/projects/lloic/files/stats/timeline.*

FIGURE 4 *A screenshot of abatishchev's version of LOIC. Retrieved from http://sourceforge.net/projects/loic/.*

FIGURE 5 *A screenshot of NewEraCracker's version of LOIC. Retrieved from https://github.com/ NewEraCracker/LOIC/.*

versions will be examined because they represented a particular line of evolution for the tool, were very often linked in media coverage and LOIC tutorials, and were extremely popular, counting by the download numbers. Both hewed closely to praetox's original code while updating the graphical user interface (GUI) and adding features. The version from abatishchev is the older of the two, initially uploaded to SourceForge in June of 2009.[16] This version of LOIC was downloaded 116,988 times in December 2010, up from 61,936 times in at the beginning of Operation Payback in September (see Figures 2 and 3). To compare, in August 2010, before the launch of the first wave of Operation Payback, this version of LOIC was downloaded 5,318 times.[17] Together, the September 2010 (when Operation Payback initially began) through December 2010 (when the Avenge Assange portion of Operation Payback took place) downloads make up nearly a third of the 567,476 downloads abatishchev's version of LOIC racked up from June of 2009 to October of 2011 (see Figure 2). Just under a third of those downloads occurred during the week of Operation Payback's Avenge Assange campaign. It is impossible to tell from SourceForge records how many of those downloading the tool actually used it during the course of Operation Payback, but it is an impressive and telling spike.

NewEraCracker uploaded his version of LOIC to GitHub in late September 2010, stating clearly that his work was based on abatishchev's version of the original praetox tool, as was written in the project's README file[18]: "LOIC—An open source network stress tool, written in C#. Based on Praetox's loic project at https://sourceforge.net/projects/loic/." Note that NewEraCracker credits Praetox but links to abatishchev's SourceForge project. From its creation in September 2010–December 2011, NewEraCracker's version of the tool was downloaded 80,660 times (unfortunately, GitHub does not currently offer finer-grain analytics on projects).[19]

Although NewEraCracker's and abatishchev's tools share virtually identical GUIs and core functionalities, there are differences in the design and functionality of each tool that would be recognized by and appeal to different participant groups. Both employ the same color scheme, dark blue on black with white text, and use the same image of a futuristic laser weapon firing at a planet, although different fonts are used for the LOIC moniker. Both GUIs are peppered with references to memes and video games that would be instantly recognizable to individuals associated with Anonymous or familiar with internet meme culture, although the references differ between the two versions in ways that make the tools temporally and politically distinct. A meme is an idea, phrase, image, or other concept that spreads virally over the internet and is adopted, repeated, and remixed by people. In Anonymous culture, many memes serve as markers of community involvement, shibboleths to differentiate those who are part of the community from those who are not. These differences can be used to position the different versions of the tool in time and how DDoS was being used by Anonymous in terms of its activist strategy. For instance, the phrase "A cat is fine, too," which appears as the default message in the transmission-control protocol/user datagram protocol (TCP/UDP) message field in the abatishchev version (see Figure 6), began appearing on 4chan and /b/ in 2006.[20] "Desudesudesu," also included in the TCP/UDP message field, references a separate meme, also popular on 4chan in 2006.[21] NewEraCracker replaces that message with "U dun goofed," a reference to the Jessi Slaughter meme, which became widespread during the summer of 2010[22] (see Figure 7). The abatishchev version also includes the subtitle "When harpoons, air strikes and nukes fail," a reference to the video game series *Command and Conquer*, from which the name "Low Orbit Ion Cannon" is taken.

One reference the abatishchev and NewEraCracker versions share in common is the "IMMA CHARGIN MAH LAZER" phrase, splashed across the button one presses to launch the attack. This references the Shoop Da Whoop meme, which also originated on the 4chan/b/board in 2006.[23] Whereas "IMMA CHARGIN MAH LAZER" and "U dun goofed" enjoyed widespread popularity beyond 4chan, "A cat is fine, too"

FIGURE 6 *In this screenshot of abatishchev's LOIC, the TCP/UDP messaging field is highlighted, with the default message, "A cat is fine too. Desudesudesu."*

FIGURE 7 *In this screenshot of NewEraCracker's LOIC, note the highlighted change in the TCP/UDP's default message, from "A cat is fine too" to "U dun goofed."*

references an obscure bestiality meme derived from Japanese manga. It did not achieve recognition or popularity beyond 4chan and similar image boards, such as SomethingAwful and YTMND. Given the proliferation of 2006 internet memes in the older versions of LOIC, and given that 2006 predates any significant media coverage of Anonymous or 4chan, it is reasonable to assume that the original developer of LOIC was most likely active on /b/ and with Anonymous, saw the target audience as members of the same community, and developed the tool sometime during 2006.

These two versions of LOIC are semiotically tagged with memes popular within different populations at the time of development. The abatishchev and, theoretically, original praetox versions reflect memes that occurred predominantly within the community of /b/ and 4chan and did not leak out into the wider internet culture. The NewEraCracker version replaced those more obscure references, either because the developer did not recognize them or because he wanted to explicitly realign the cultural references of the tool with memes that had attracted the attention of the more mainstream internet culture. At the time, the Jessi Slaughter "U dun goofed" meme had attracted the attention of popular internet culture blogs, such as Gawker, and the mainstream news media.[24] So marked, NewEraCracker's version of LOIC can be seen as appealing more to individuals who had relatively little interest in the more recreationally offensive aspects of /b/'s culture but were drawn to Anonymous for other, perhaps predominantly political, reasons. This shift in rhetorical tone can also be interpreted as a reflection of Anonymous' overall move away from its 4chan roots, toward a new activist identity.

The changes made by NewEraCracker also heighten the explicit and overt political value of the tool. Whereas "A cat is fine, too" and "Desudesudesu" are relatively nonsensical in the context of an adversarial DDoS attack, "U dun goofed" is explicitly confrontational. It accuses the target of making a grave error and implies that he or she is now, or shortly will be, suffering the consequences of his or her actions. In the original viral video from which the meme sprang, "U dun goofed" is followed shortly by the line "The consequences will never be the same."[25] So whereas the praetox and abatishchev LOIC can be seen as calling out to a specific, rather limited group of like-minded individuals, the NewEraCracker LOIC throws its net much more broadly and advertises its vengeful motives much more overtly. This messaging functionality is identical to the one found in the original FloodNet tool. The message many never be seen by the target and, as such, serves more as a rhetorical flourish for the benefit of the sender, adding a weight that might not be carried by the hurling of bits alone, and augments the sense of communal participation.

The design of the interface makes the operation of the tool relatively simple, even for someone with little experience participating in DDoS actions, but it also contains features for more advanced users to "personalize" their actions. The required steps (target, attack mode, and some customizable options) are numbered one through three. A website can be targeted by entering either its URL or its IP address. A more advanced user can also set the port destination, the number of simultaneously open threads, request timeout, and the relative speed with which packets are hurled at the target. Most of these options have a default setting, so all an inexperienced user has to do is enter a target URL, click "IMMA CHARGIN MAH LAZER," and sit back. However, if a user were still confused, there are a myriad of tutorials and FAQs available online, posted on webpages and as video tutorials on YouTube. Information on how to operate LOIC is, and in December of 2010 was, extremely easy to find. In fact, much of the news coverage of Operation Payback and Operation Avenge Assange contained enough information to constitute a tutorial on the use of LOIC in and of itself.

A significant difference between the abatishchev and NewEraCracker versions of LOIC is NewEraCracker's addition of the Hive Mind automated attack mode (see Figure 8).

This added functionality also represents an important advancement from FloodNet, which, like abatishchev's LOIC,

FIGURE 8 *In this screenshot of NewEraCracker's LOIC, note the addition of "FUCKING HIVE MIND" and attendant options at the top of the interface.*

operated in only one "manual" mode. Although the tool automated the process of sending packets, a user still had to target and engage the tool manually. Hive Mind mode allowed the tool be controlled remotely, through the IRC[iii] protocol. During Hive Mind mode, the user was essentially volunteering his or her machine to be part of a botnet, wherein many different machines were controlled by one. To operate in this mode, the user simply selected "Hive Mind" at the top of the interface and entered the IP address of the IRC server, the port number, and the channel name. These were also set to defaults during installation, further simplifying the process. Moreover, nearly all of Anonymous' internal communications during the December stage of Operation Payback took place in IRC channels, so it is very likely that even a relatively new participant would be passingly familiar with its protocols. But again, if a user were confused, there were and still are many tutorials to be had just a Google search away.

The Hive Mind feature represents a significant break with the one-person/one-computer protocol practice exemplified by FloodNet. Although an original goal of the FloodNet project might have been to "leave one's computer protesting at home and then hit the streets to do the same,"[26] it was Anonymous that actually took advantage of the protocol's physics-defying potential. Hive Mind mode enabled Anonymous to engage with participants who did not, for whatever reason, follow the targeting and scheduling information that Anonymous was constantly releasing and updating. A lower level of commitment was required. Although Anons may not have "hit the streets" as EDT envisioned, Hive Mind mode did enable them to go to school, work, sleep, or anywhere while still participating in DDoS actions as they arose. Hive Mind mode was not the

---

[iii]IRC, or Internet Relay Chat, is an internet protocol to support instant messaging, chat, and synchronous conferencing. IRC channels are hosted on a central server and joined by individuals via clients or an online interface. Hive Mind exploited the IRC protocol to control an instance of LOIC on a given machine.

first time an activist DDoS campaign used volunteer botnets. An earlier instance, the Help Israel Win campaign in 2008, is examined in the next section.

By updating and making more accessible the memes in the tool's interface, and by adding functionality that allowed less technically able individuals to participate in the actions, Anonymous was able to expand its participant community dramatically. Coleman quotes one Anon as saying that the number of participants on the Operation Payback IRC servers rose from an average of 70 participants to over 7,000. The ease with which one could participate in the Operation Payback actions was rivaled only by the ease with which one could take on the identity of an Anon. As noted previously, the Anonymous identity meme is based on the strengthening of a central core via the participation of many individuals who move in and out of different active or passive states. This subsumption of personal agency has the potential for a strong biographical impact on the participants, particularly, those who had not previously considered themselves political actors, by merging their agency with other active participants. This merging allows for the temporary sharing of an activist identity, which subsequently becomes more easily adopted by those participants who opt to remain involved.

Changes in the technology

It is becoming increasingly difficult for a purely volunteer, manual style DDoS action (which require a body in a chair for the duration of the action and can claim the strongest line of symmetry to physical-world sit-ins) to have a noticeable effect on a large, robust corporate website. Advances in technology as well as the vending of DDoS defense services to at-risk sites by companies like Akamai and Arbor Networks mean that even automated, strictly volunteer-supported DDoS actions are unlikely to cause downtime. This had led to the use of botnets, traffic multipliers, automated tools, and other exploits to bring the power of such actions in line with the defenses employed by targets. While the use of such technological tools doesn't automatically negatively affect the validity of an activist DDoS action, the use of nonvolunteer botnets is a particularly worrying turn. Volunteer botnets present their own ethical concerns, but are less immediately objectionable.

Another aspect to consider is how advances in infrastructure and connectivity have changed the nature of DDoS actions over time. Groups like Strano, the EDT, and others active in the 1990s and early 2000s structured their actions to be of short duration, 2 or 3 hours at most. The Strano Netstrike action, which took place on December 21, 1995, lasted for only an hour.[27] The EDT's "Tactical Theater Schedule," a list of the FloodNet actions taking place in 1998, notes that actions run from "10:00 a.m. to 12:00 p.m. and 4:00 to 6:00 p.m . . . Mexico City Time" for each of the thirteen dates listed.[28] The technical and financial realities of dial-up internet prevented, for the most part, more ambitious actions of longer duration. *The electrohippies'* 1999 WTO action was unique in that it was designed to take place continually over a number of days. The November 29, 1999 call-to-action e-mail states, "The sit-in will begin 08.00 USA & Canada (Pacific time) 30th November . . . and will finish four days later."[29] The e-mail notes that those with dial up connections may not be able to stay online for the whole planned 4 days, and so advises:

If you cannot afford to spend much time online then concentrate on November 30th (or Dec. 1rst for those in the East). But we would like people to aim to go online for 12.00 Pacific time on December 3rd (add 4 hours to the above timetable for your local time) until the end of December 4th.[30]

The transition from telephone-based internet connections to broadband, DSL, cable, and fiber connections has altered the duration calculus for DDoS actions. With the high speed, always-on internet connections available to many participants, DDoS actions have the potential to go on for days, or weeks, or indefinitely. While organizers were once constrained simply by technical capacity, other concerns, including ethics, must now come into play when determining the duration of DDoS actions.

In addition to the Hive Mind supported volunteer botnet, there were several large nonvolunteer botnets involved in Anonymous' Operation Payback.[31] Nonvolunteer botnets are created by infecting computers with a program that allows them to be controlled by a remote server without the owners' knowledge. The use of someone's technological resources without their consent in a political action, particularly one that carries high legal risk, is a grossly unethical action. Moreover it cheapens the participation of the activists who are consensually participating, and makes it easier for critics to dismiss DDoS actions as criminality masquerading as free speech.

Prior to Anonymous' Hive Mind powered volunteer botnets, the tactic had been used by pro-Israeli activists in 1999. A group of Israeli students calling themselves Help Israel Win released a tool that allowed people to participate in DDoS actions, ostensibly targeting anti-Israel websites. Like LOIC's Hive Mind mode, individuals who downloaded the Patriot DDoS software package from help-israel-win.tk could link their computers to an IRC server and participate in DDoS actions. Unlike LOIC, Patriot runs solely in the background and does not allow for user input of any kind.[32] The original website is no longer online or archived, however Jeffrey Carr quotes the group's self-characterization as "a group of students who are tired of sitting around doing nothing while the citizens of Sderot and the cities around the Gaza Strip are suffering."[33] Their goal of "unit[ing] the computer capabilities of many people around the world . . . in order to disrupt our enemies efforts to destroy the state of Israel"[34] echoes similar sentiments articulated by *the electrohippies* around their WTO action.

The release of the tool itself garnered a moderate amount of media attention, attracting coverage in *Wired*[35] and blogs.[36] The *Wired* article notes that at one point there were roughly 1,000 computers hooked into the botnet, and Help Israel Win claimed credit for bringing down sarayaalquds.org and qudsvoice.net.

Volunteer botnets also raise issues of consent, ones which are incumbent on the organizers to address. Volunteer botnets make it easy for different people to participate in DDoS actions without encountering the hardships that sitting in front of a computer and searching for targeting and scheduling information might present to working individuals, students, or people in different time zones than the primary organizers. By participating in a volunteer botnet, they can pledge their support and resources to a given cause and trust the organizers to utilize those resources wisely. This then places a responsibility on the organizers to maintain strong, open communications channels with those participants and not make significant changes to the operation of the DDoS campaign without their consent. It is also necessary that organizers publicize information on how one might withdraw from a voluntary botnet if one should wish to do so.

Notes

1   Jordan and Taylor, *Hacktivism and Cyberwar*, 87.

2   Dominguez, "Electronic civil disobedience," 1807.

3   Jordan and Taylor, *Hacktivism and Cyberwar*, 81.

4   Ibid.

5   Nate Anderson (2010), "Operation Payback attacks to go on until we 'stop being angry,'" *Ars Technica*, September 30, 2010. Last accessed February 27, 2014, http://arstechnica.com/tech-policy/news/2010/09/operation-payback-attacks-continue-until-we-stop-being-angry.ars.

6   Anderson, "Operation Payback attacks."

7   Gabriella Coleman, *Hacker, Hoaxer, Whistleblower, Spy: The Story of Anonymous* (Brooklyn, NY: Verso Forthcoming).

8   Anderson, "Operation Payback attacks."

9   David Kravets, "Exclusive: I Was a Hacker for the MPAA," *Wired*, October 22, 2007. Last accessed February 27, 2014, http://www.wired.com/politics/onlinerights/news/2007/10/p2p_hacker?currentPage=all.

10 Anderson, "Operation Payback attacks."

11 Correll, "Tis the season of DDoS."

12 Coleman, "Our weirdness is free."; Parmy Olson, *We Are Anonymous* (New York, NY: Little Brown, 2013).

13 Quinn Norton, "Anonymous 101 part deux: Morals triumph over lulz," *Wired*, December 2011. Last accessed February 27, 2014, http://www.wired.com/threatlevel/2011/12/anonymous-101-part-deux/all/1.

14 Coleman, "Geek Politics and Anonymous."

15 Christina Warren, "How Operation Payback executes its attacks," *Mashable. com*, December 9, 2010. Last accessed February 27, 2014, http://mashable.com/2010/12/09/how-operation-payback-executes-its-attacks/.

16 Relevant development dates and other statistical information on the abatishchev version of LOIC are available from the LOIC project page on SourceForge, http://sourceforge.net/projects/loic/.

17 abatishchev LOIC SourceForge project page.

18 The README file for NewEraCracker's version of LOIC is available at https://github.com/NewEraCracker/LOIC#readme.

19 These statistics are available on the NewEraCracker GitHub project page, https://github.com/NewEraCracker/LOIC.

20 Know Your Meme, "A cat is fine, too," *Know Your Meme*, 2009. Last accessed February 27, 2014, http://knowyourmeme.com/memes/a-cat-is-fine-too.

21 Know Your Meme, "Desu," *Know Your Meme*, 2009. Last accessed February 27, 2014, http://knowyourmeme.com/memes/desu.

22 Know Your Meme, "Jessi Slaughter," *Know Your Meme*, 2010. Last accessed February 27, 2014, http://knowyourmeme.com/memes/jessi-slaughter.

23 Know Your Meme, "Shoop da whoop," *Know Your Meme*, 2009. Last accessed February 27, 2014, http://knowyourmeme. com/memes/shoop-da-whoop-i%E2%80%99m-a%E2%80%99- firin%E2%80%99-mah-lazer.

24 Know Your Meme, "Jessi Slaughter."

25 Ibid.

26 Dominguez, "Electronic civil disobedience," 1810.

27 Julie Thomas, "Ethics of Hacktivism," SANS Institute, January 12, 2001. Last accessed February 27, 2014, http://www.giac.org/ paper/gsec/530/ethics-hacktivism/101266.

28 This schedule is currently archived at http://www.thing. net/~rdom/ecd/ecd98.html and was last accessed April 23, 2013.

29 ehippies@tesco.net, "WTO Sit-in open!"

30 Ibid.

31 Olson, *We Are Anonymous*; Gabriella Coleman, *Hacker, Hoaxer, Whistleblower, Spy: The Story of Anonymous* (Brooklyn, NY: Verso, forthcoming).

32 Jeffrey Carr, *Inside Cyber Warfare* (Sebastropol, CA: O'Reilly Media, 2011), 28.

33 Carr, *Inside Cyber Warfare*, 28.

34 Ibid.

35 Noah Shachtman, "Wage Cyberwar Against Hamas, Surrender Your PC," *Wired*, January 8, 2009. Last accessed February 27, 2014, http://www.wired.com/dangerroom/2009/01/israel-dns-hack/.

36 Ethan Zuckerman, "Install a trojan for Israel? Uh, no thanks," *My Heart's in Accra*, January 18, 2009. Last accessed February 27, 2014, http://www.ethanzuckerman.com/blog/2009/01/08/ install-a-trojan-for-israel-uh-no-thanks/.

CHAPTER SEVEN

Against the man: State and corporate responses to DDoS actions

Confrontational activism, like activist DDoS, is a conversation with power, often state or corporate power. Activists make a statement or take a stand, and the response of the state or corporate target often has a strong impact on the perceived success or even legitimacy of the activist action. Responses to activist DDoS actions by states and corporations have varied widely over the years the tactic has been in use. In at least one case, the case of Andreas Vogel, a court of law has declared DDoS actions to be valid forms of activism and condoned their use as a tool of collective action. In others, as we shall see, the judicial response has not been nearly so sympathetic, resulting in high fines, significant jail time, and other costs for participants.

This chapter is an attempt to place the responses of corporate and state entities to activist DDoS actions in context within several trends in the regulation and governance of the online space. The attempts to turn the internet into a business-friendly marketplace noted by the EDT and *the electrohippies* have not abated. In recent years and months, these regulatory efforts in support of the business community (both in the United States and abroad) have been augmented by attempts to make the internet "surveillance-friendly" on a technological level, turning the online space into a zone open to monitoring by state organizations looking to root out terrorism, as well as those with in an interest in turning the online space into a legitimate field of warfare. These interests have melded with those of the pro-business sector, and the result has been a collision of corporate and state efforts to lockdown nontraditional uses of technology and to heavily discourage vocal and visible displays of disruption and dissent. This, combined with the issues of politically legitimating media coverage covered earlier, result in a legal, cultural, and technical environment that chills the development of innovative technological outlets for political action and speech.

Terrorism accusations and the CFAA

In their DDoS action against the WTO in 1999, *the electrohippies* were, in many ways, operating within a self-generated frame of digital activism. Though they were attempting to adapt the accepted frame of civil disobedience from physical-world activism, the ways in which they were attempting to apply that frame to their disruptive, direct action campaign against the WTO were novel. This framing, that disruptive, distributed dissent, which occurred often at a physical and sometimes political distance,[i] was necessary for the validation of distributed activism that occurred primarily in the online space. Recognition of this frame was needed for *the electrohippies*' actions to be viewed as legitimate activism. Unfortunately, as was noted earlier, this often did not happen, as *the electrohippies* themselves note:

> As a result of the WTO action *the electrohippies collective* were labeled as terrorists. . . . The problem with the knee

---

[i]Most of the organizers and activists in *the electrohippies* were British and operated from the United Kingdom.

jerk response of politicians and e-commerce gurus is that we run the risk of losing legitimate electronic action as governments use the excuse of "hackers" to criminalize certain activities. We must make sure that both the positive and negative aspects of internet activism are clearly debated, and that cyberspace is not excised from the everyday realm of constitutional rights and freedoms.[1]

This classification mostly took place in the media. Other analysts, such as Dorothy Denning, paid greater attention to groups' self-characterization:

While the above incidents were motivated by political and social reasons, whether they were sufficiently harmful or frightening to be classified as cyberterrorism is a judgment call. To the best of my knowledge, no attack so far has led to violence or injury to persons, although some may have intimidated their victims. Both the EDT and *the electrohippies* view their operations as acts of civil disobedience, analogous to street protests and physical sit-ins, not as acts of violence or terrorism. This is an important distinction. Most activists, whether participating in the Million Mom March or a Web sit-in, are not terrorists. My personal view is that the threat of cyberterrorism has been mainly theoretical, but it is something to watch and take reasonable precautions against.[2]

Denning's testimony before the House Armed Services Committee, combined with *the electrohippies*' statement, highlights a number of issues pertinent to the influence and roles of states in digital protests. While Denning acknowledges the role of self-identification in judging the activist value of an action, *the electrohippies* point out that if the online space as a zone is judged to be unavailable for activist action, then the self-identification matters little. As the internet developed from a pseudopublic academic intra-net into a vital part of everyday life for many people, it was inevitable that those who opposed the privatization of a perceived commons would be systematically marginalized by both the corporate and state interests that stood to benefit financially and politically from stabilization of the network. So, although Denning hangs her definition of terrorism on the hook of personal harm and violence, she also acknowledges that a "judgment call" is required when classifying new disruptive behaviors.[3] When the relevant "judge" is also the target of the disruptive protest, it is in their interests to reclassify legitimate protest as ideological violence.

There have been several cases of activist DDoS actions that have gone to trial or been pleaded out, in the United States and internationally. A significant case is that of Andreas-Thomas Vogel, a German national who ran the libertad.de website during the 2001 Deportation Class action against Lufthansa Airlines. Vogel had posted a call to action on libertad.de and was arrested on charges on coercion. Initially in 2005, a lower court in Frankfurt found Vogel guilty of using force against Lufthansa, based predominantly on the economic losses the airline had suffered during the campaign, both in terms of lost sales and the costs of acquiring additional bandwidth to soak the protesters' traffic. Vogel was sentenced to either pay a fine or serve 90 days in jail. However, the next year, a higher court overturned the verdict, finding, ". . . the online demonstration did not constitute a show of force but was intended to influence public opinion."[4] Libertad responded to the ruling with a statement that echoed those we have seen from *the electrohippies* and the EDT: "Although it is virtual in nature, the Internet is still a real public space. Wherever dirty deals go down, protests also have to be possible."[5]

The Vogel case was the first international precedent to recognize the legal and philosophical arguments put forth by supporters of DDoS activist actions. The court decision pivots on the point that these actions were oriented to influence the public, and through that avenue, influence the actions of the Lufthansa corporation, rather than badgering the airline into conceding to a set of demands. Specifically, the judge ruled that the protest was not an action of force intended to compel an action from Lufthansa; the action's intention was to impact public opinion first.

There has been no such precedent-setting case thus far in the US courts. This is in part due to the limited number of arrests resulting from DDoS actions until recently, and such cases very rarely make it to trial. Two individuals were arrested in connection with Anonymous' Operation Chanology DDoS actions against the Church of Scientology in 2007 and 2008. Both cases resulted in guilty pleas.[6] One, Dmitri Guzner, was sentenced to serve 366 days in federal prison and pay $37,500 in restitution to the Church of Scientology.[7] The second, Brian Thomas Mettenbrink, also served a year in prison and was ordered to pay $20,000 in restitution to the church. Eric J. Rosol, a Wisconsin truck driver, participated in a DDoS action against the Koch Industries website in 2011, running LOIC for approximately 60 seconds.[ii] He pleaded guilty in December 2013 to one misdemeanor count of accessing a protected computer, and was sentenced two years' probation and ordered to pay $183,000 in restitution to Koch Industries, a multinational conglomerate which reported revenues of over $115 billion in 2013.[8] The Operation Payback DDoS actions resulted in 14 individuals (including one minor) being charged under the CFAA with participating in the DDoS action against PayPal. Each defendant was charged with two felony counts, which could have resulted in up to 15 years in prison and fines of up to $500,000.[9] In early December 2013, the PayPal14 struck a deal. Of the 14 individuals charged, 11 pleaded guilty to one felony count of conspiracy and one misdemeanor count of damaging a protected computer, and agreed to pay $5,600 in restitution to PayPal. Two others from the group pleaded guilty to the misdemeanor only, and were sentenced to 90 days in prison as well as the $5,600 restitution payment. The final

---

[ii]As a result of the collective action Rosol participated in, which was part of a larger protest against the governor of Wisconsin's move to strip public employees of their collective bargaining rights, the Koch Industries website was inaccessible for approximately 15 minutes.

defendant faced a concurrent indictment for charges stemming from another Anonymous action, and was ineligible for the plea deal. Others have been convicted in connection with the action internationally.[10]

Potential sentences for DDoS actions in the United States are high compared to other crimes and especially compared to other types of traditionally recognized activist activities. For example, in the United States a sit-in would typically result in charges of trespass, if anything. In the state of Massachusetts, the punishment for criminal trespass is "a fine of not more than one hundred dollars or imprisonment for not more than thirty days or both such fine and imprisonment,"[11] substantially lower than the terms agreed to by the PayPal14 deal. Resisting arrest, another typical charge, results in a term of imprisonment of up to "two and one-half years or a fine of not more than five hundred dollars, or both."[12] DDoS actions are prosecuted under Title 18, Section 1030 (a)(5) of the US Code, otherwise known as the CFAA. DDoS actions, along with other computer crimes, and are classified as fraud. US sentencing guidelines, laid out yearly in the United States Sentencing Commission Guidelines Manual, which are used as recommendations regarding federal cases within the US legal system, contain a series of adjustments that can be applied to a "base offense level" according to a number of factors. The resultant "offense level" is then used to determine the recommended sentence. Particularly relevant to the case of DDoS actions are those adjustments that involve the amount of financial losses suffered[13] and the number of victims.[14] PayPal claimed in a British court that the Operation Payback action cost them £3.5 million in losses, or roughly $5.5 million.[15] That loss figure would add 18 levels to the base offense level for fraud of 7. PayPal did not disclose in court the number of victims it believes was impacted by Operation Payback, but we can assume it was probably higher than 250, which is the maximum listed in the US Sentencing Guidelines, for an additional 6 offense levels, giving us a total offense level of 31. For an individual with no previous criminal record, the recommended sentence for an offense level of 31 is 135 months, or more than 11 years. This is without the "special skills" or "sophisticated means" adjustments, both of which would add several more offense levels.

A "special skill" is defined by the US Sentencing Guidelines as "a skill not possessed by members of the general public."[16] "Sophisticated means" is defined as "complex" or "intricate offense conduct pertaining to the execution or concealment of an offense."[17] Whether or not these enhancements are applied depends heavily on the discretion, and the technical sophistication, of the judge handing down the sentence. To someone with little experience with computers or the internet, directing your web traffic through a proxy may count as "sophisticated means" of concealment, and running an IRC channel or even just running LOIC may constitute a "special skill." This means that, for now, individuals arrested for crimes involving computers are at particular risk for being sentenced based not on what they actually did, but based on how little the arbiters of justice know. In instances where those individuals know and understand little about the technical specifics of the actions before them, they are more likely to fall back on cultural stereotypes and media depictions to make their judgment. Though internally Anonymous may delight in the bad-boy-hacker and Internet Hate Machine images the media uses to describe them, in a court of law the hacker-as-folk-devil figure makes it more likely that activists, mischief-makers, and even researchers will be treated as dangerous members of a criminal elite.

There are no established requirements for determining the figures for losses or number of victims in these cases. PayPal and the prosecution stated during the UK trial of Christopher Weatherhead that they included the "considerable damage to its reputation and loss of trade" that resulted from the actions in their calculations.[iii] In Rosol's case, the $183,000 figure came

---

[iii]Weatherhead was sentenced to 18 months' jail time for his role in Operation Payback, which did not include participating in the actual DDoS actions.

not from the actual financial losses the company reported to the court, which amounted to less than $5,000. Rather, Koch Industries claimed the DDoS action resulted directly in their hiring a consulting firm to improve their web infrastructure, at a cost of $183,000.

Because the CFAA is fraud statute, charges filed give plaintiffs the ability to extract restitution from defendants as part of the resulting criminal judgment. This is in addition to the criminal fines described in the sentencing guidelines. In 46 out of the 50 US states, defendants may also be subject to joint and several liability, which means that in the event a plaintiff is found to have been injured by more than one person, the plaintiff can recover all of their damages from one defendant, regardless of that defendant's individual liability. Joint and several liability enables plaintiffs to shift the burden of liability distribution and collection to the defendants, while the plaintiff quickly recovers damages from a single party. Joint and several liability is how Eric Rosol found himself liable for Koch Industries's $183,000 consulting bill. It is also the reasoning behind Dmitri Guzner's $37,500 restitution payment to the Church of Scientology, and Brian Thomas Mettenbrink's $20,000 payment. In these cases, the use of joint and several liability is imposing a devastating and chilling cost on individuals for their participation in a collective action. The line of causality is clear: participate in an act of collective civil disobedience online, and run the risk of being held liable for hundreds of thousands of dollars in damages. Trespass, resisting arrest, or disorderly conduct, charges that most commonly result from on-the-street collective action, are not legally formulated in the United States to result in victims who have the ability to extract damages from a defendant. When used to prosecute activist DDoS actions, the CFAA directly gives the targets of protest the ability to extort payments from activists for their dissent and disruption. When coupled with the innovative reality of online activism, the CFAA literally renders the internet a space where you can be charged hundreds of thousands of dollars for participating in a collective protest.

The CFAA is a bad law for many reasons, but there are specific aspects to it that make it particularly ill-suited to handle collective online political actions. The lack of oversight in the calculation of damages and the low maximum number of victims mean that the judicial system is predisposed to come down hard on the participants and organizers of these actions. Threats of long prison terms and extreme fines lead to most individuals pleading out before trial, which could delay a precedent-setting court decision such as the Vogel decision in Germany, which could legitimate disruptive civil disobedience online in the United States. "Special skills" and "sophisticated means" sentencing enhancements exacerbate the lack of technical knowledge among members of the judiciary and can easily result in substantially more severe sentences for defendants. Finally, the liability structure created by the CFAA, coupled with joint and several liability, creates a system by which the targets of protest and dissent can impose direct costs for that dissent on activists, creating a massive chilling effect on digital activism as a whole.

GCHQ's rolling thunder and the (re)militarization of the internet

That DDoS actions are widely considered illegal has not stopped states from using the tactic as a tool of harassment, censorship, or cyberwarfare. In breathtaking displays of hypocrisy, states have been known to target DDoS actions against those groups that have faced prosecution for running their own activist DDoS actions.

In February 2014, journalist Glenn Greenwald and others at NBC released a story based on some of the files released by NSA leaker, Edward Snowden.[18] The story revealed that the

Government Communications Headquarters (GCHQ), the British signals intelligence and information assurance agency, had launched a series of exploit-based DoS actions[iv] against Anonymous IRC servers and engaged in other attacks against the online resources of hacktivist groups. The operation, known as Rolling Thunder, targeted the IRC channels used by Anonymous with the intention of disrupting communication and potentially scaring away participants. By some estimates, the server disruption lasted for over 30 hours.[19]

This is not the first time state forces have explicitly launched "hack back" attacks against digital activists. In September of 1998, the Pentagon responded to an EDT FloodNet action by unleashing a piece of countermeasure code called "Hostile Applet," which causes any browser running the FloodNet program to crash.[20] A *Wired* article quoted a Defense Department spokesperson as saying, "Our support personnel were aware of this planned electronic civil disobedience attack and were able to take appropriate countermeasures. . . . Measures were taken to send the countless demands [from the attacker's servers] into the great beyond."[21] The appropriateness of the Pentagon's response was questioned at the time. There were questions as to whether the US military should be deploying "cyber-attacks" within the United States even as a "defensive measure," or against civilians.[22] The "hostile applet" was arguably the first use of military-grade "cyberweapons" against civilians, but it comes in a long line of military technology being deployed to control protest and dissent in the US. This history includes the use of barbed wire for human containment in the 1800s, tear gas for crowd control in the 1920s, rubber bullets and beanbag projectiles in the 1970s, and military-grade pepper spray being adopted for regular police use in the 1990s.[v] More recently,

---

[iv]From the information available at the time of writing, it appears that this was not technically a *distributed* denial of service action, but rather an exploit-based action using a technique called an SYN flood.

[v]I am indebted to Professor Anna Feigenbaum of Bournemouth University for explaining this history to me.

the Long Range Acoustic Device (LRAD) sonic weapon was deployed at the 2009 G20 meeting in Pittsburgh, Pennsylvania to control and suppress street demonstrations. The LRAD creates a focused beam of sound that can reach up to 150 decibels, and can cause instant, incapacitating headaches and permanent hearing loss at a range of 100 meters.[23] While the use of military technology like the "hostile applet" to stifle a political protest was hardly new, it signaled an intention on the part of the US Department of Defense to extend the military-style policing of dissent from the streets to the internet.

The revelations about GCHQ's Rolling Thunder operation have met with strong criticism as well. As Gabriella Coleman wrote in *Wired*, one doesn't have to agree with the political goals or tactics of Anonymous to conclude that it is a deeply hypocritical abuse of power for states to attempt to disrupt the activities of activists using tactics that the state itself has declare illegal and worthy of prosecution. Coleman writes, "When Anonymous engages in lawbreaking, they are always taking a huge risk in doing so. But with unlimited resources and no oversight, organizations such as the GCHQ (and theoretically the NSA) can do as they please. And it's this *power differential that makes all the difference*."[24] Coleman points out that the Rolling Thunder denial of service actions disrupted the activities of thousands of Anonymous participants, many of whom were not even involved in the Operation Payback DDoS actions. The GCHQ specifically and intentionally disrupted the rights to speech and assembly of thousands of individuals.

When used by political activists, disruptive tactics like DDoS actions can act as power levelers: they enable activists to funnel media and public attention to unnoticed causes and events, and as direct action tactics DDoS actions allow activists to translate their political speech into an action which demands a response. Disruptive tactics are valuable to those underfunded or unpopular causes that sit outside the mainstream of attention and support. The power to disrupt is vital to the potential of these causes and their supporters to be influential in the world. GCHQ and the Pentagon don't need the power to disrupt the organizing activities of activists with impunity in order to be influential in the world. By using these tactics, organs of state power such as the GCHQ colonize them, making them less appealing, less useful, and less effective for dissident groups. They alter how the use of those tactics will be received by the media, the public, and the political community.

The use of these tactics, declared illegal for use by any other type of actor, is deliberate. I argue that the use of these tactics in the name of law enforcement and national security is a deliberate move to extend the Hobbesian state monopoly on force to include code that states see as "offensive" or "weaponized." This could include DDoS tools, DoS exploits such as the SYN flood used by the GCHQ, scripts to scrape large amounts of data from a website or server, or any other chunk of code that could be used for a disruptive, destructive, or perhaps simply nontraditional purpose. As more bits of code and uses of technology can be removed from the public domain and monopolized by the state as part of its war-fighting domain stable, online actions that were previously innocuous, irritating or even criminal can be reclassified as the tools and tactics of war. The internet can be progressively classified as a valid war-making space, or even as an active battlefield. Where *the electrohippies*, in their worst case scenario, saw a creeping marketplace mind-frame ready to transform the internet into a capitalistic wonderland, the use of SYN flood DoS actions by the GCHQ, and the Pentagon's "Hostile Applet" before that, could portend the establishment of a semipermanent state of cyberwar, with any potentially disruptive code held by states as monopolized "cyberweapons." A state of active cyberwarfare existing anywhere on the network could substantially increase levels of surveillance, while expansive definitions of what counts as "weaponized code" or "cyberweapons" could result in the widespread classification of civilians as "cyberterrorists" or enemy combatants.

The internet as melded commercial/military space

The dual forces of commercialization and the defense interests of states have combined to foster an online environment that is increasingly hostile to innovative or disruptive modes of political engagement and dissent. State security and commerce have become blended concerns, each supporting the other both in furtherance of their goals and in the construction of their mutual enemies. Anna Feigenbaum has traced what she calls an "elision . . . in which social welfare and the protection of commerce become joint enterprises—solvable only through integrated alliances between government and business."[25] This elision of goals also combines means and targets: ". . . the conflation of cybercriminals and cyberterrorists works to legitimate forms of surveillance, policing and prosecution that infringe individuals' civil liberties and apply terrorism legislation against a wide range of the population, particularly political protesters."[26] Feigenbaum goes on to note examples of corporate executives, such as Sony's Kaz Hirai, offering a view of the world which conflates crimes against individuals and actions which rock the infrastructural stability that online commerce relies on. "Under this logic," Feigenbaum concludes, "the anti-capitalist protester can be easily understood as a criminal, and at times, a 'domestic extremist' or 'domestic terrorist' . . ."[27]

Beyond the ways in which corporate and state security interests have been conflated lies the very real manner in which corporations and other commercial entities have taken a strong, some might say primary role, in governing the online space, both through influence over traditional, state level regulatory agencies and multinational organizations and agreements, but also through direct, "ground level" tools such as terms of service user agreements and more subtle choices at the levels of code and interface design. Because of this, many corporations, most of which provide services that are "invisible" to the user, such as content delivery networks, operate as de facto governance entities in the online space. But these are not governance entities for which the public's rights of participation, protest, or dissent are fully legally or even culturally established. Rather, it would appear that the online space is being or has already been abdicated to a capitalist-commercial governance structure, which happily merges the interests of corporate capitalism with those of the post-9/11 security state while eliding democratic values of political participation and protest, all in the name of "stability." The manner in which the public may engage discursively, productively, and politically with entities that disclaim status as governmental entities yet whose actions and policies clearly have distinct governmental impact in the online space has not yet been settled. We are left with a collection of corporately structured governmental entities that cannot be meaningfully talked to, using the language of a discursive democracy.

Some can hardly be talked to at all. As an example, in the summer of 2011 Google rolled out a "real name policy" on Google+, a social network deeply embedded in the constellation of Google products, and in July 2011 began suspending accounts that did not use (or did not appear to use) legal names. This caused widespread criticism over Google's seemingly arbitrary decisions as to what constituted a "real" name, and their apparent refusal to consider the reasons why people may not want to use their legal names on public social networking services, including reasons of privacy and personal safety.[28] However, Google didn't (and still doesn't) have an "ombudsman" or "community manager"-type individual to whom users could reach out with their concerns or negative experiences. Google waited till October 2011 to announce that it would begin supporting pseudonyms.[29] However, at this time, the Google+ "Create Your Google+ Profile Name" page, as of February 2014, still states, **"First and last name required:** You need to provide both your first and last name for your Google+ profile so it'll help you find people and enable people to find you. Using only one name is not permitted," and requires users who use mononyms to go through a lengthy appeals process.[30] Despite crows of victory[31] from groups like the EFF at Google's October 2011 announcement, it is far from clear that Google has reconsidered their stance on real names or seriously considered the concerns of those who objected to the policy. By not meaningfully adjusting their policy in the face of reasonable and well-founded criticism, or even fully following through on a pledge that they would, Google demonstrates the unaccountable nature of the influence they wield in the online space and over the actions and abilities of those individuals who spend time there.

This has left us with a catch-22. There are no meaningfully accessible democratic channels through which to communicate dissent or protest to these entities, as they have functionally used the structures of corporate capitalism to opt out of the processes of discursive democracy. But attempts to express dissent and protest through disruptive activism or other innovative digitally based tactics are attacked as not belonging to the stable of popularly acceptable protest tactics, or condemned as criminal or terroristic departures from democracy. The functional advantage of a DDoS in this de-democratized context lies in how it serves a translation function, turning the democratic language of a collective action into the loss/gain, signal/silence, on/off language of these techno-capitalist governance entities.

The avatar nature of online brand presence

DDoS actions expand potential modes of interaction between individuals or groups of individuals, and techno-capitalist corporations. Corporate websites allow for a symbolic and actual centralizing of the normally distributed brand reality of a corporate entity. Just as a corporate headquarters acts as the physical-world manifestation of a corporation's brand identity, and individual products as distributed, appendage-like instances of the same, a company's website functions as a digital, responsive brand model, but as a cohesive whole. In physical-world activism, the activist is restricted to confrontations with the physical manifestations of corporate brands, which, especially in the case of national or multinational entities, are often only a part or appendage of the whole corporate entity. Instances of activism are limited in their scope and impact: a defaced billboard is still just one among many; an action at a factory or headquarters does not distribute itself across multiple brand enactments. But because a corporate brand website is meant to represent a sprawling corporate entity as a coherent, comprehensible whole, a confrontation with that digital entity is effectively symbolic of a confrontation with the corporation as a whole. The bounded nature of the website allows a new, more symmetric manner of confrontation with individual activists, bounded individual to bounded individual. The vulnerability of the single instantiation empowers the activist for the duration of the confrontation, rather than the corporation.

As holistic representations of corporate entities, websites are high value brand manifestations. As such, interference or disruption of predictable continuity can provoke a response that other activist tactics are unlikely to elicit. By imbuing corporate websites and digital, branded storefronts with the symbolic selfhood of avatars, corporations have effectively reduced their public resilience to be equal only to the resilience of that website. Downtime, instability, or even poor design can lead to a poor public opinion of the company itself. The symbolic investment of corporate selfhood in these online presences should not be interpreted as either reducing the ability of the corporation to exploit other lines of public communication (through spokespeople, press conferences, etc.) or as permission to reduce the actual and legal vulnerability of such corporate avatars to disruption and disparagement, either through DDoS actions, parody, satire, or appropriation. Mickey Mouse may be precious to Disney, but (for now, at least) he can still be used as a tool of derision against his parent company. Any crack in that digital facade requires immediate attention, as it has the potential to reflect on the entire corporation, not just one part. In its pre-internet, distributed incarnation, any number of slights, insults, or disruptions could have gone unremarked upon. But as a website now can be the manifestation of an entire corporate entity or brand, continuity disruptions cannot be disregarded. Again, this necessity-of-response empowers activists by acting as a forcing function with regard to the responses of corporations. Rather than having to wait and hope that corporations will respond to an activist action, with the very likely result that the action will simply be ignored, offenses to the sanctity of the digital brand representation come too close to disrupting the image of corporate continuity and stability to be ignored. By virtue of the symbolic value they have invested in the digital brand representation, corporate entities have obligated themselves to engage with the public disruption, thus providing activists with a trigger point, provoking a public response.

Like states, these responses are often an attempt to push an interpretation of the actions as criminal or antisocial rather than activist in nature. As stated earlier, it is relatively easy for corporations to claim large damage and victim totals, thus making it appear that these actions are more disruptive and destructive than they may actually be. By overestimating their potential for damage, corporations can promote the perspective that DDoS actions are incompatible with the continued presence of legitimate business on the internet.

In the face of this, the question arises: why go for the symbolic disruption of a corporate homepage when core systems, such as PayPal's payment processing systems might have been disrupted instead? This response echoes the critiques of the CAE, namely that attention-oriented activism, or activism which aims to influence media and public opinion first, is not as effective as direct action models. This criticism, however, does not consider that there may be multiple, equally viable goals to an activist DDoS campaign, and that not all goals are equally served by simple, covert disruption. If the goal is to publicize, say, PayPal's participation in Wikileaks Banking Blockade, disrupting their payment processing system does little to further that goal. This goal is markedly different than attempting to disrupt the internal operations of an already high-profile event like the WTO. Within an analysis of a disruptive action, the nuances of what is disrupted and how are relevant. In some cases, it is more useful to disrupt an image, while in others it is more useful to disrupt a process.

Notes

1 DJNZ/electrohippies, "Client-side Distributed Denial-of-Service."

2 Dorothy Denning, "Prepared Statement of Dorothy E. Denning Georgetown University Before the House Armed Services Committee Oversight Panel on Terrorism," *Federal News Service*, May 23, 2000. LexisNexis.

3 Denning, "Prepared Statement."

4 "Higher Regional Court says online demonstration is not force," Heise Online, June 2, 2006. Originally published at http://www.heise.de/english/newsticker/news/73827, currently Archived at http://post.thing.net/node/1370. Last accessed February 27, 2014.

5 Hans-Peter Kartenberg, quoted in *Heise Online*, "Higher Regional Court."

6 Dan Goodin, "US teen admits to 'Anonymous' DDoS attack on Scientology," *The Register*, October 17, 2008. Last accessed February 27, 2014, http://www.theregister.co.uk/2008/10/17/scientology_DDoS_guilty_plea/; John Leyden, "Second man jailed over Scientology DDoS attacks," *The Register*, May 25, 2010. Last accessed February 27, 2014, http://www.theregister.co.uk/2010/05/25/second_scientology_DDoSer_jailed/.

7 Associated Press, "Dmitriy Guzner: Teen Sentenced in Scientology Cyber Attack," *Huffington Post*, November

18, 2009. Last accessed February 27, 2014, http://www.
huffingtonpost.com/2009/11/18/dmitriy-guzner-teen-
sente_n_362713.html.

8 Ryan J. Reilly, "Loading Koch Industries Website Too Many
Times In 1 Minute Just Cost This Truck Driver $183,000,"
Huffington Post, December 2, 2013. Last accessed February
2014, http://www.huffingtonpost.com/2013/12/02/anonymous-
koch-attack_n_4374365.html.

9 Curt Hopkins, "Anonymous to show up in person for 'PayPal
14' trial," *The Daily Dot*, February 28, 2013. Last accessed
February 27, 2014, http://www.dailydot.com/news/anonymous-
rally-paypal-14-court-trial/.

10 Chloe Albanesius, "Anonymous Hacker Gets 14 Months for
PayPal, MasterCard Attacks," *PC Magazine*, January 24, 2013.
Last accessed February 27, 2014, http://www.pcmag.com/
article2/0,2817,2414674,00.asp.

11 Massachusetts General Laws, Part IV, Title 1, Chapter 266,
Section 120: "Entry upon private property after being forbidden
as trespass; prima facie evidence; penalties; arrests; tenants or
occupants excepted. Retrieved from http://www.malegislature.
gov/Laws/GeneralLaws/PartIV/TitleI/Chapter266/Section120.

12 Massachusetts General Laws, Part IV, Title 1, Chapter 268,
Section 32B: "Resisting arrest." Retrieved from http://www.
malegislature.gov/Laws/GeneralLaws/PartIV/TitleI/Chapter268/
Section32b.

13 United States Sentencing Commission Guidelines Manual,
2B1.1.b.1, (2012).

14 United States Sentencing Commission Guidelines Manual,
2B1.1.b.2 A-C, (2012).

15 Sandra Laville, "Anonymous cyber-attack cost PayPal
£3.5m, court told," *The Guardian*, November 22, 2012. Last
accessed February 27, 2014, http://www.theguardian.com/
technology/2012/nov/22/anonymous-cyber-attacks-paypal-court.

16 US Sentences Commission Guidelines, 354.

17 Ibid., 94.

18 Mark Schone, Richard Esposito, Matthew Cole, and Glenn
Greenwald. "War on Anonymous: British Spies Attacked

Hackers, Snowden Docs Show," *NBC News*, February 4, 2014. Last accessed February 27, 2014, http://www.nbcnews.com/news/investigations/war-anonymous-british-spies-attacked-hackers-snowden-docs-show-n21361.

19 Schone et al., "War on Anonymous."

20 Meikle, *FutureActive*, 153.

21 Niall McKay, "Pentagon Deflects Web Assault," *WIRED*, September 10, 1998. Last accessed February 27, 2014, http://www.wired.com/politics/law/news/1998/09/14931.

22 Meikle, *FutureActive*, 154.

23 "The future of crowd control," The Economist, December 2, 2004. Last accessed February 27, 2014, http://www.economist.com/node/3423036.

24 Gabriella Coleman, "The New Snowden Revelation Is Dangerous for Anonymous—And For All of US," *WIRED*, February 4, 2014. Last accessed February 27, 2014, http://www.wired.com/opinion/2014/02/comes-around-goes-around-latest-snowden-revelation-isnt-just-dangerous-anonymous-us/.

25 Anna Feigenbaum, "Security for Sale! The visual rhetoric of marketing counter-terrorism technologies," *The Poster* 2 (2011): 85.

26 Feigenbaum, "Security for Sale!" 85.

27 Ibid., 86.

28 For an overview of the Nymwars, Eva Galperin's article, "2011 in Review: Nymwars," provides an excellent, well-linked starting place, available at https://www.eff.org/deeplinks/2011/12/2011-review-nymwars.

29 Greg Finn, "Google+ To Allow Pseudonyms & Will Support Google Apps Accounts," *Search Engine Land*, October 20, 2011. Last accessed February 27, 2014, http://searchengineland.com/google-to-allow-pseudonyms-will-support-google-apps-accounts-97825.

30 "Create your Google+ profile name," 2014. Last accessed February 27, 2014, https://support.google.com/plus/answer/1228271?hl=en.

31 Eva Galperin, and Jillian, C. York, "Victory! Google Surrenders in the Nymwars," *Electronic Frontier Foundation Deep Links Blog*, October 19, 2011. Last accessed February 27, 2014, https://www.eff.org/deeplinks/2011/10/victory-google-surrenders-nymwars.

Conclusion: The future of DDoS

Over the course of this book, I've attempted to arrive at a thorough description of the history and current practice of activist DDoS actions. The question now is, will the practice of activist DDoS actions continue, or are practical, theoretical, and ethical challenges faced too great to allow for the tactic to be effective?

As I described earlier, downtime is notoriously hard to achieve for an all-volunteer activist DDoS action, especially against a large corporate target. An "arms race" dynamic has ensued, which encourages the use of nonvolunteer botnets and exploits to augment volunteer efforts and which also diminishes the ethical validity of activist DDoS actions. The defensive capabilities of for-hire firms such as Akamai, Prolexic, and Arbor Networks, responding mainly to the advancements in criminal DDoS actions, continue to outstrip the capabilities of nearly all activist campaigns.

As downtime continues to become more and more difficult to ethically achieve, media exhaustion also becomes a concern. In 2013, criminal DDoS actions received more coverage than activist DDoS actions, and coverage often does not make clear the distinctions between the two types of actions. Could activist DDoS actions simply become invisible in the sea of criminal actions? Or could the media landscape go the other way, with DDoS actions of all stripes becoming so commonplace that they warrant no coverage at all? Either outcome would be devastating for the publicity and messaging goals of activist DDoS actions.

The use of DDoS as a tactic of extortion, criminality, and nation-state initiated censorship is damaging to its perceived legitimacy as an activist tactic. This association hampers the perception of activist DDoS actions as legitimate and worthwhile acts of political activism, and also prevents the further diffusion of the tactic. The flamboyant, antisocial pantomime performed by Anonymous and other similar groups further restricts *open* use of the tactic to an online fringe.

Because of its enduring associations with criminality and extreme online subcultures, in addition to its current legal status and particular technical challenges, I think it is unlikely at this time that DDoS actions will ever become a part of the popularly accepted activist repertoire of contention in the near future, unlike similar physical-world tactics like sit-ins or occupations. However, I predict that DDoS actions will remain popular among internet-based fringe groups and subcultures, particularly those that adhere to a Barlowian view of the independent, self-contained nature of the internet. As high-profile hacker and computer crime cases come to trial these will serve as radicalizing events, "group grievances," for the transgressive, technologically mediated subcultures that are currently serving as cultural laboratories for disruptive online activism.

This radicalization, which occurs most strongly in the aftermath of convictions (such as those of Andrew Aurenheimer, also known as weev; or Jeremy Hammond) or tragedies (such as the suicide of Aaron Swartz), further underlines the perceived disjuncture between behavioral norms in these subcultures (or, in some cases, in more mainstream, technologically sophisticated populations) and the legal response delivered by the state. The popular association of activist DDoS actions with criminality is often not of interest to these radicalized groups, and may even be a point of attraction. The disapproval of the state can serve to underscore its cluelessness with regard to the internet and technologically mediated transgressive subcultures, a cluelessness that these subcultures in turn often see as something to mock and exaggerate.

Is the use of DDoS by these groups abridging their ability to develop other innovating forms of online activism? The answer to this is an unequivocal "no." Though not examined in this book, the resurgence of tactics like doxing, "human flesh search," information exfiltration, leaking, defacement, software development, the remote organization of backup internet connectivity in the event of nation-level shutdowns, alternative infrastructure and service construction, and large-scale data analysis, either automated or human-distributed, are all indicators of innovative developments in tactical and strategic activism. However, many of these are advanced activities, requiring significant skill, organization, support, and planning to pull off. They are not entry-level activities. As such, the pool of potential participants is much smaller, and would not necessarily benefit from a massive influx of inexperienced but nonetheless eager participants. Moreover, many of the tactics listed earlier and others are not attention-oriented in the same way that many activist DDoS actions are: massive amounts of media attention are not their goal, and may be detrimental. The attention-oriented nature of activist DDoS actions lends itself to encouraging media coverage at a level that other tactics might not.

As a "street-less" space, that the internet runs counter to many assumed practices of speech and public politics appears to belie Nathan Jurgenson's "digital dualism" fallacy.[1] The "speechy" nature of the online space had led to this seeming contradiction, wherein existing speech online is so highly valued that we drastically devalue other types of disruptive, activist speech which are tolerated, even specifically valued, in the off-line world. If we acknowledge that civil disobedience and disruptive activism are valuable tools of activist speech and political discourse in the physical world, than it must also be acknowledged that they should be equally valuable and desirable in the online space. In the online space, dissenting speech should have a platform and a voice, ones that we are occasionally obligated to encounter, just as we encounter them in the physical world. As an avenue for speech, the internet should also be open to dissenting, potentially disruptive speech. Without forced encounters with dissent, our democratic society will stagnate.

Activist DDoS actions started as an exploration into the activist potential of the internet by activists experienced in street activism. In its modern incarnation, activist DDoS is practiced mainly by fringe actors, who consider the online space a primary zone of interaction, socialization, and political action. Though in many ways an extremely accessible stepping stone to more involved methods of online activism, DDoS actions remain privileged in many ways, including their basic technological nature, the specific populations involved, and the specific legal and cultural challenges inherent in modern nonmainstream computer use. Though DDoS itself may become increasingly marginalized as an activist practice, high-profile campaigns such as Operation Payback and the ensuing legal battles have opened the debate on the validity, desirability, and potential of disruptive activism and civil disobedience in the online space. This book is presented as a step toward the robust analysis of these repertoires of contention in the online space that has become such an integral part of our modern culture.

Note

1   Nathan Jurgenson, "Digital Dualism versus Augmented Reality," *Cyborology*, February 24, 2011. Last accessed March 3, 2014, http://thesocietypages.org/cyborgology/2011/02/24/digital-dualism-versus-augmented-reality/.

INDEX

BIOGRAPHIES

Molly Sauter is a PhD student in Communication Studies at McGill University in Montreal, Canada. She holds a Master's in Science from MIT, USA, in Comparative Media Studies.

Foreword by:

Ethan Zuckerman is Director of the Center for Civic Media at MIT, and a Principal Research Scientist at MIT's Media Lab. He is the author of *Rewire: Digital Cosmopolitans in the Age of Connection* (2013) and co-founder of the international blogging community Global Voices.